The
STEAMBOAT
REVOLUTION

LONDON'S FIRST STEAMSHIPS

THE
STEAMBOAT
REVOLUTION

LONDON'S FIRST STEAMSHIPS

TIM SHERWOOD

TEMPUS

First published 2007

Tempus Publishing Limited
The Mill, Brimscombe Port,
Stroud, Gloucestershire, GL5 2QG
www.tempus-publishing.com

British Library Cataloguing in Publication Data.
A catalogue record for this book is available from the British Library.

ISBN 978 0 7524 3894 8

Typesetting and origination by Tempus Publishing Limited.
Printed in Great Britain.

Contents

Steamboat *Nymph*.

PREFACE

Steamboats, which were often elegant and picturesque, launched mass tourism. For the two decades from 1820, they were an extremely important form of transport. The story in this book is about the sea-going steamboats operating from London: services to Gravesend (a resort visited by one million tourists a year at its peak), Margate and Ramsgate (both upmarket resorts). These ships had dining rooms, and bands played the popular numbers of the time. The steamboats to Hull and Edinburgh, and the continental services to Germany, Holland, Belgium and France had not only dining rooms but cabins with beds too.

The period covered is roughly 1815 to 1860. I have not included the story of the heavily used downriver services to Woolwich and Greenwich, and the upstream services to places such as Richmond and Kingston. They have been described elsewhere. The subject of steamboats is badly documented (in comparison to railways, for example) which explains why historians have avoided it, so the reader is entitled to be more than usually sceptical about some of the information here. Charles Dickens, at the peak of his powers in the 1830s and 1840s, used the steamboats and was fascinated by the Thames; his descriptions are of such luminous clarity that it is impertinent to try and improve on them and they are therefore quoted at length.

Who else used this new means of travel? It attracted everybody who could afford the fares (which came down as time went on): the aristocracy (who could also take, not only their servants, but their horses and carriages as well), the commercial and professional classes, and the growing numbers of mechanics, tradesmen, clerks, musicians, actors, and entertainers of every kind. Many, but not all, travelled with their wives, mothers, daughters, sisters, and girlfriends, not to mention women travelling on their own. Some passengers found it better to leave their families behind. Mingling with them would have been all sorts of people on the make: courtesans, thieves, tricksters and various impostors. The steamboats were used by celebrity writers such as W. M. Thackeray and Samuel Taylor Coleridge, and the painter J.M.W. Turner, in addition to Dickens. There was a kaleidoscope of tourists from the Continent; the antics of these adventurers are an essential part of the story. The steamboats carried Londoners, so the book has descriptions of the early nineteenth century City, and the Pool of London.

As with many new inventions, the steamboats were at first greeted with disbelief and fear. There were boiler explosions and fires but, as the technology improved, public confidence grew. Dramatically, they raced each other down the Thames, and constantly swamped smaller craft. Collisions were commonplace. The steamers were strongly resented by the London watermen, whose livelihood was jeopardised.

ACKNOWLEDGEMENTS

For help with this book I have pleasure in thanking Robert Poulter, John Williams, and Michael Berlin. Michael read the script in the early stages and suggested important changes. Captain George Hogg, RN, of the National Maritime Museum, Cornwall, kindly read a later draft and made valuable suggestions. I also have pleasure in thanking the curator of the Margate Local History Museum; members of the Margate Local History Society, especially Mick Twyman; Mike Hunt of the Ramsgate Maritime Museum, and Colin Middlemiss of The Company of Watermen & Lightermen. I would also like to thank Arthur Credland of Hull Maritime Museum, and the librarians and archivists at the National Maritime Museum, the National Archives, Guildhall Library, Museum in Docklands (London), Tower Hamlets Local Studies Library, Gravesend Library, the library at London's Transport Museum, and Putney Library. Finally, Dick Wood and Bruce Rankin for help with pictures, and Fay Miller who suggested improvements in style. Any mistakes are entirely my responsibility.

LIST OF ILLUSTRATIONS

CHAPTER ONE

INTRODUCTION

Steam navigation has within the last twenty years, effected a great revolution as to the time employed in traversing distances, and consequently a great revolution in society.[1]

At the beginning of the nineteenth century it was simpler to bolt a steam engine in to the hull of a ship than to install one on a wheeled vehicle. The wooden paddle steamer, or steamboat, was therefore the first successful application of steam technology to transport. It became a very important means of travel before the railway arrived. The heyday of the steamboat was from 1820 to 1850. It provided coastal and Continental services. This book is about this forgotten but significant enterprise, which affected the lives of millions of people because it made mass tourism possible for the first time in history. The steamboat revolution provided a new and better, and certainly cheaper, means of transport for all the reasons that people wanted to travel, whether for a day's outing, a weekend, a holiday, visiting families or friends, or for work. It lasted until the railways came. Although steamboats started trading from major ports such as Liverpool, Hull, and Glasgow, this investigation is confined to the impact and consequences of the steamboat on Londoners. It is not concerned with the technical development of the steamboat, but with the social impact of this form of transport.

From the Pool of London, services evolved to the Kent coast (mainly for tourism), the East Coast, to Scotland, the English Channel ports, and to Dublin. The steam services to the Continent, the forerunners of today's car ferries, were for both commerce and tourism. The growth of services was impressive: in 1820 there were nine steamboats operating from London; by 1830 there were fifty-seven. There was a similar increase in the use of steam propulsion at Liverpool, Hull, and Glasgow. By 1842 sixteen steamers

THE SALOON STEAM-PACKET COMPANY'S VESSEL ALEXANDRA, FOR PASSENGER TRAFFIC ON THE THAMES.

The Saloon Steam Packet Co.'s vessel *Alexandria*, for passenger traffic on the Thames.

were taking one million Londoners each year, to the fashionable saltwater resort of Gravesend. Gravesend is an example of a resort which prospered and expanded due to the steamboat.

On the coastal services the steamboat replaced parallel stagecoach services because it could carry more passengers and was therefore cheaper and, particularly in summer, was far more comfortable. Meals and sleeping accommodation were provided. On the East Coast from Margate to Edinburgh, a quarter of a million passengers were carried each year in the 1840s. The steamboat was safer and more seaworthy than the sailing ship, and because it was less affected by wind and tide, a meaningful timetable could be offered for the first time in maritime history. At first the steamboat services were used by the upper and middle classes, but with declining fares and increasing prosperity they came to be patronised by the lower–middle and artisan classes: shopkeepers, tradesmen, mechanics, and clerks. The steamboat, because of its reliability, was suitable for carrying mail, currency, bullion, light valuables, and light perishables such as dairy products. The steamboat also came to carry livestock. An important and profitable role was towing: by 1840 there were twenty-three steamboats towing sailing ships in and out of the Pool of London. The steamboat was of shallow draught (generally 12–14ft), and was manoeuvrable because the wheels could be reversed independently; it was eminently suitable for rivers and estuaries. Its limitations were due to the undeveloped engines which consumed vast amounts of coal: large quantities had to be carried which took up revenue-earning space on board, and supplies had to be provided at all ports. Coal, the price of which fluctuated, represented, on average, about 25 per cent of the owner's costs. Another limitation was, predictably, weather: services, especially for tourism, were curtailed in winter, though when services were possible, they were run. Advertisements in the newspapers of the time testify to this. Some of the routes were of a speculative nature – Herne Bay being an example – but for the owner, the ship was a capital asset on which the optimum return was needed. There was flexibility in that it could be chartered to other owners.

The supremacy of the sailing ship in carrying heavy bulk cargo – iron, coal, bricks etc remained until the last quarter of the nineteenth century. By then the development of efficient engines enabled the steamship to prevail, but by that time the coastal passenger trade had been reduced by the railway. It is true to say that early wooden steamships were a symbol of the new, modern, world. Yet they were located in the old world – the Romantic Age before the railways came. The steam locomotive was a representation of the new world, and when it came it supplanted the stagecoach, and eventually replaced the coastal passenger steamer.

NOTES

1 24 July 1841, *Herapath's Railway Magazine,* p.623.

2 For example *The Times* in October, November and December 1836, January 1837 and December 1840.

CHAPTER TWO

BEFORE 1815

During the later eighteenth century 'taking the waters' at the seaside had become increasingly fashionable, and was boosted by the appearance of George III bathing at Weymouth in 1789. Seaside resorts outstripped spas and later 'gradually changed from health centres to havens of pleasure'.[1] Those who could not afford transport walked to the coast and became known as 'trippers' – the term dates from 1813.[2]

Margate was first advertised as a resort in 1736, coincidentally the same year as the first marine steam engine was patented, and became a fashionable watering-place between 1750 and 1770.[3] It was not as famous as Bath, but it had the sea, which Bath did not, and seawater was becoming the alternative panacea to spa water. When doctors started recommending seawater, it was not always apparent whether an 'exhausted dandy' should swallow it or bathe in it.[4] But bathing and drinking seawater are still considered good for eczema and scurvy and other skin complaints. In order to provide privacy when undressing as close to the water as possible, bathing machines were introduced. Furthermore, in 1796, the Sea Bathing Infirmary was opened at Margate which, by 1850, had dealt with 22,000 patients.[5] Medical pamphlets explained when seawater would be beneficial:

> In cases of langour and debility, hysterical affections, epilepsy, St Vitus's dance, convulsions in children…bathing at proper times, has been found remarkably efficacious.[6]

Despite the advance of medical knowledge there is, of course, still no cure for some of these ailments and gradually sea bathing changed from a medical ritual to a recreation. Nevertheless, the sea and its ozone continued to be regarded as healthy, as now, and must have been a great relief from the severely polluted air of London.

Margate Hoys – various images were produced of them and this is one of the more restrained. *Commercial postcard, painting by S. W. Forbes, 1795. Margate Local History Museum*

Commodities such as corn and fish had been transported by sea from Margate to London during the eighteenth century, and possibly earlier. One-masted vessels of 60–100 tons called *hoys*, a generic term possibly of Danish origin, had been employed in this trade. In response to demand, some of them were adapted to carry passengers in the 1790s. The hoys could carry sixty to seventy or even 100 passengers – the evidence varies. By 1800 it was estimated that they carried 20,000 passengers to Margate in one year. Essentially they were open barges, of which there were many in the Thames. By any standard the conditions on these vessels were extremely primitive; little shelter was provided, and only a few beds were installed, which, it seems, were used by many of the passengers in rotation. One (unknown) writer called the hoys a 'floating jail', and they were popular targets for satire. One of the most alarming features for the time was the mixing of classes, as well as the sexes. But in calm, dry and warm weather the sea voyage would have been pleasant. Charles Lamb is full of nostalgia for them in *Essays of Elia*.

They could take ten hours or three days depending on tides and weather. Their main attraction was the low fare: the evidence varies between 2s 6d[7] and 5s[8]. The other advantage of the hoys was that they could carry a considerable amount of luggage. They had few accidents and were therefore considered safe, if not comfortable. The stagecoaches took about fifteen hours for the journey – which made for a long day over uneven roads. They were not, of course, so seriously affected by bad weather, but they were also uncomfortable (all travel was), especially for the outside passengers. The fare ranged expensively from 21s (outside) to 26s (inside) – which was at least four times higher than the hoy.

Although the journey could be stressful and exhausting, doctors regarded sea-sickness as beneficial for some complaints. Better still were the diversions to be had, as Lord Campbell recorded:

> My fellow passengers were pretty numerous, but so exactly resembling those represented by the satirists of the age to be found on board, that it would be mere commonplace to describe them or their behaviour. I had a flirtation with a cheesemonger's daughter who was going to Margate with her mamma, but she was too suddenly loving, and I went off in disgust. There was scarcely a breath of wind, so that it was low water before we had got far below Gravesend.[9]

In any event, the demand for passenger travel to Margate grew. The vessels were given hopeful and optimistic names, intended to instil confidence in the passengers, such as *Endeavour, Fortune,* and *Good Intent.* The introduction of steamboats reduced the number of sailing hoys required (by 1822 there was only one passenger hoy left) but did not eliminate them. Their role as carriers of bulk commodities and mixed cargoes continued. In the 1840s three cargo hoys were working between London and Margate, and passenger demand increased to the point where two passenger hoys re-entered service – though probably not for long.

And what of Gravesend? In the eighteenth and nineteenth centuries it was a popular seaside resort. For Londoners the best way to get there was by the river, on the 'Long Ferry' as it was called. The service was provided by *tilt* boats – a sailing wherry in which the passengers had cushioned seats in the after part and were protected by a canvas awning. These departed from Wapping and Billingsgate. In the 1720s Daniel Defoe remarked that so many people travelled by the 'great ferry' between London and Kent that the volume of traffic was 'hardly credible', yet he was disparaging about Gravesend, saying that it had 'nothing considerable in it'.

Despite the uncertainty and discomfort of the hoys, *The Times* could report on 16 September 1797 that 'so great is the rage for watering places, that the Margate packet had, the week before last, 152 passengers on board'. Likewise, *The Observer,* three years later, on 24 August 1800, could report that 'seven hoys last week conveyed to Margate 1,342

Seawater bathing. Satirising the fashion for seawater bathing by the greatest satirist of the age, Thomas Rowlandson (1756–1827). *Guildhall Library. Catalogue no. ?*

persons'. By 1802 nine of them were carrying over 20,000 passengers to and from Margate during the summer season. It had been reported earlier that:

> Margate is now, through the smiles of a generous public, become a populous thriving town. There are upwards of 700 families resident in the town, exclusive of the great number of visitants who annually spend some of their summer months in this place.[10]

The affordability of travel to Margate by sea meant that it lost its exclusivity *before* the introduction of the steamer: the lower-middle classes (clerks, shopkeepers, tradesmen, and artisans) started arriving in the 1800s. Indeed the rough and tumble of a voyage on a hoy could not have been agreeable to the refined middle classes: a Margate guide of 1789 actually said that 'very few persons in genteel life come by water'. Possibly Lord Campbell was more daring than he seemed. But some middle-class men (and their servants) braved the hoys and sent their womenfolk by stagecoach.

Notes

1 Brendon, *Thomas Cook*, p.11. At the same time doctors regarded fresh air as harmful.

2 *Ibid*.

3 Girouard, *The English Town*, p.83.

4 Cruickshank, *Charles Dickens and Early Victorian England*, p.16.

5 Walton, *The English Seaside Resort*, p.20.

6 Whyman, *Kentish Sources VIII, The Early Kentish Seaside (1736-1840)* (Gloucester 1985), p.156, (EKS). WC Oulton, *Picture of Margate and its vicinity* (Second edition 1821), p.54.

7 Garwood, *Thames Steamers*, p.5.

8 Whyman, *Water Communications to Margate and Gravesend as coastal resorts before 1840. Southern History, vol. 3* (1981), p.114 (*SH*).

9 General Information on Hoys and Steamboats. One wonders what he meant by saying that she was 'too suddenly loving and I went off in disgust'. Strong words. Later, Lord Campbell, as Lord Chief Justice, campaigned for the introduction of the Obscene Publications Act 1857, to which there was some resistance, and which subsequently caused considerable problems of interpretation. For a discussion on this see *Victorian Babylon* by Lynda Nead, pp.150–161.

10 Whyman *EKS*, p.87.

CHAPTER THREE

1815 – A TURNING POINT: THE FIRST STEAMSHIPS

The plans for the first marine steam engine were patented by Jonathan Hulls in 1736, but so far as is known, he did not construct a steamship. Later in the century the Duke of Bridgewater conducted experiments for towing barges on canals, and in 1781 the Marquis de Jouffroy built a steamboat at Lyons with which he made successful experiments on the river Saone. In France his work was not developed but experiments were carried out in Scotland, where William Symington constructed a steamboat which moved through the water at 5mph in 1788. In 1803, Symington constructed a more advanced steamboat, the *Charlotte Dundas*, which demonstrated the practicability of steam propulsion. It towed two other vessels of seventy tons each, over a distance of nineteen miles against a strong head wind. Incredibly, it was consigned to the scrapheap because the canal owners were afraid that the banks would be washed away. The *Charlotte Dundas* rusted away at its moorings.

Development continued with the construction of the *Comet* (twenty-five tons) by Henry Bell in 1811, on the Clyde. She was powered with a 4hp engine. The success of this steamboat inculcated confidence and the number of steamers gradually increased: in 1813 there was a steamboat on the Avon running between Bath and Bristol; by 1816 there were steam vessels on the Trent, the Tyne, the Ouse and Humber, Orwell, Mersey, and the Thames.

A steam vessel left the Clyde in the winter of 1814–15, sailed through the Forth & Clyde Canal, and down the East Coast to the Thames.[1] This was the *Margery* (seventy tons), named after her first owner's daughter (some sources spell the name *Marjory*) and she was the first steam vessel ever seen on the Thames.[2]

From 23 January 1815 she was run for the season between London and Gravesend. It was hardly the best month of the year to start, but was announced by the following advertisement:

The public are respectfully informed that the New London Steam Packet *Margery*, Captain Cortis, will start precisely at 10 o'clock, on Monday morning the 23rd, instant, from Wapping Old Stairs, near the London Docks, to Milton, below Gravesend, and will return from thence, at the same hour on the succeeding morning to the same stairs; the said packet having superb accommodations. Passengers and their luggage will be conveyed to and fro, with more certain speed and safety, than by any other conveyance by water or land, and on reasonable terms.[3]

The *Margery* was unreliable and was withdrawn at the end of 1815. The critical development for steam propulsion on the Thames was the arrival of the *Duke of Argyle* (seventy-four tons and 12hp) in May of 1815. Under the command of Captain Dodd she made an epic passage from the Clyde down the West Coast, calling at Dublin and Milford Haven. She put in to St Ives and called at Plymouth and Portsmouth from where she reached Margate. From there she completed the ninety-mile passage to Limehouse in nine hours. She carried fifteen tons of coal consuming an average of one ton for every 100 miles. At each port she had created immense interest, not least with the Royal Navy. The overall performance, particularly in the open sea, of this astonishing little vessel stimulated steamship building, particularly on the Clyde, Mersey and Humber. The potential of steam propulsion from London to Margate had been clearly demonstrated, which was then promoted by Sir Marc Brunel (the father of Isambard Brunel) and others.[4]

This astonishing little vessel was re-named *Thames*, and opened a service from London to Margate on 3 July 1815. She was bought by the newly-formed London & Margate Steam Packet Co. (the first steamboat company and subsequently known as the 'Old' Margate Co. as distinct from the 'New' Margate Co. of the 1830s) and sailed from Wool Quay close to Custom House (in the Pool of London) twice weekly. The new service was advertised in *The Times* four days later (7 July) assuring travellers that the vessel had:

…the special advantage of proceeding either by sails or steam, and separate engines, by which means the public have the pleasing certainty of never being detained on the water after dark… which must have been unpleasant, especially in bad weather, and frequently happened with sailing ships.

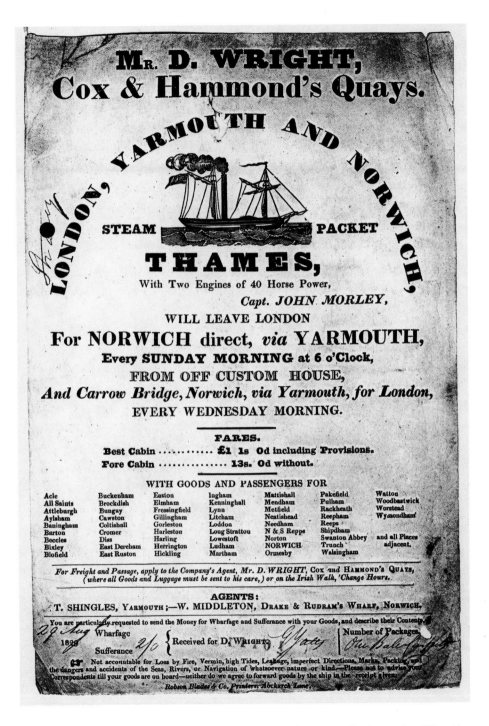

A handbill of 1829 for the steamboat *Thames*, advertising the service between London, Yarmouth, and Norwich, the cathedral city of East Anglia. *Author's collection*

According to Jackman, based on contemporaneous evidence, there were three steamboats in 1816 plying between London and ports 'as far out as Margate'.[5] These were the *Margery*, *Defiance*, and *Thames*. The *Majestic* was brought into service in 1816 and had the distinction of being the first steamer to be used for towing, when she towed an Indiaman, the *Hope*, from Deptford to Woolwich at three knots against the wind. This was to become an important role for the steamboats.

The *Regent* (112 tons) was built by Courthope of Rotherhithe and was thus the first steamer to be built on the Thames, inaugurating a new and important industry. She was designed by Marc Brunel[6] and fitted with two engines of 24hp, on either side of the boiler, by Maudslay of Lambeth. On trials she steamed from Blackfriars Bridge to Battersea Bridge in thirty minutes, and back through London Bridge in fifty-two minutes.[7] The *Regent* replaced the *Thames,* which was transferred to the Gravesend service, and was the first to undertake day excursions, which rapidly became popular. However, the *Regent* came to grief: her funnel was blown off causing the wooden base to catch fire. At the time she was between Whitstable and Reculver with forty passengers, but her captain succeeded in beaching her without loss of life.

Steam services were starting on the Mersey to Ireland, as well as on the Clyde and Humber, but weaknesses in design and equipment meant that accidents and boiler explosions were not uncommon, causing public concern. A House of Commons Select Committee was therefore appointed in 1817 to investigate, which led to legislation providing for the inspection and registration of steamers. Indeed the new invention was frightening to many people. A waterman recalled his reaction to the first steamboat he encountered:

> …I recollect very well coming up the Pool, in a fog, in 1814, in a fishing smack, and hearing the noise of the first steam–vessel I ever saw. We were all of us plaguey frightened on board. The noise of the steam blowing off, and the beat of the paddles, produced a very terrible effect in the darkness.[8]

This suggests that there may have been a steamboat on the Thames before 1815 – but the waterman may have got his date wrong. There is a record of a more extreme reaction on the Clyde, which is quoted by John Kennedy. When being overtaken by the *Comet*, the captain of a Clyde sloop piped 'all hands – a man and boy' and bade them: 'Kneel down and thank God that ye sail wi' the Almichty's ain win', and no' wi' the deevil's sunfire an' brimstone, like that spluttery thing there.'[9]

As the steamboats developed and their performance improved they gained acceptance and popularity; a succession of vessels appeared, each larger than their predecessors. Sir

Rowland Hill, of penny postage fame, whilst having a summer holiday at Margate witnessed the arrival of a steamer:

> We went to see the steamboat come in from London. It is worked by means of two wheels, resembling water-wheels, one of which is placed on each side of the vessel, and about half-sunk in the water. It comes from London and returns three times in each week. It generally performs the voyage in about twelve hours. In the best cabin there is a handsome library, draught-boards, etc. It is surprising to see how most people are prejudiced against this packet. Some say that it cannot sail against the wind if it is high; but when it entered the harbour the wind and tide were both against it, and the former rather rough, yet I saw it stem both. There was a great crowd, and much enthusiasm, though carpers predicted failure, and sneered at 'smoke-jacks.'[10]

The early paddle steamers, the steamboats, were basically wooden sailing ships into which a boiler and engine was installed, consisting of a boiler and firebox, and cylinder (one or two?) with paddles fitted to each side of the hull in casing of approximately 15ft diameter. At least half the wheel was above deck level. Angle irons were used to strengthen the hull. The length was approximately 80ft with a 12–15ft beam. There were upward-sloping bows, with a figurehead, a projecting bowsprit, two or three masts. Forward was the fore-cabin, and at the stern was the first or chief cabin – later called the saloon. Each was entered by a steep stair which was protected by being boxed in and enclosed by a door above deck.

Dominating their appearance was a tall smokestack of about 25ft which had the owner's marking on it as it was so prominent, a practice which continued until recent times. The height of the funnel kept the smoke clear of the master and the passengers, and also created a draught in the firebox. There was also a single square sail. The name of the vessel was on the bow or on the paddle box. A considerable amount of space would have to be given up for coal, and although there is no mention of it in the literature, fresh water for the boiler would also have to be carried. The steam pressure in the boiler was about 25psi – low in order to avoid the risk of explosion, and about the same as with early railway locomotives. Because of the high capital and running costs, the fares, at 15s for the after cabin and 11s for other cabins, were pitched at a higher level than for the sailing hoys at 2s 6d to 5s, but were still substantially less than the coaches at 21s to 26s. What was unprecedented was the provision of genteel entertainment whilst travelling, such as backgammon, and draughts, and also a library. Food and drink was on offer. As an inducement to upper- and middle-class women it was announced that:

For the express purpose of combining delicacy with comfort, a female servant attends upon the Ladies.[11]

Although most passengers would sit in the saloon, there were private cabins, at extra cost, available. They were luxurious, especially in comparison to any form of travel before: 'to be compared to a London coffee house.' Steamers on the Continental trade, on the Hamburg route, experimented with coal-gas lighting.[12] There were criticisms of the 'unpleasant monotony' of the motion (which must have been a gentle swell), and 'the constant vibration of the timbers'.[13] As they developed and increased in size, the cost of building steamers rose from around £10,000 in 1817 to £20,000 in 1825.

Charles Dickens' fertile imagination was stimulated by the Thames and as we know he became a regular user and observer of the steamboats. He found that the revolutionary technology excited strangers to such an extent that they could talk to each other without being introduced:

'Wonderful thing steam, sir.'

'Ah (a deep drawn sigh) it is indeed, sir!'

'Great power, sir.'

'Immense – immense!'

'Great deal done by steam, sir.'

'Ah! (another sigh at the immensity of the subject, and a knowing shake of the head) you may say that, sir.'

'Still in its infancy they say, sir.'[14]

Despite teething problems, the steamboats were unquestionably a success, simply because they were far faster than sailing ships, and far more reliable. Even in the summer of 1815 the *Gentleman's Magazine* had reported that the *Thames* was 'much thronged with passengers'.[15]

The years 1815 to 1820 form the heroic phase of the wooden paddle steamer. This consisted of great achievements accompanied by frequent mechanical breakdowns, accidents, and boiler explosions, as already noted. In 1817 a passage to the Continent was completed: the *Caledonia* (423 tons), which had been the first steamboat on the Humber three years previously, steamed from Margate to Rotterdam at an average speed of seven and a half knots, and sailed up the Rhine to Cologne.[16] Therefore reliability was improving and confidence growing in steam propulsion, but safety standards and levels of expectation were far lower than they are today; out of 760 ships registered, forty steamships were wrecked, twenty-three suffered boiler explosions, and seventeen experienced fires from various causes in the period 1829–1839.[17]The steam locomotive railways in the 1830s and 1840s were not free from boiler explosions.

Notes

1 Jackman, *The Development of Transportation in Modern England,* p.455.

2 *Ibid.*

3 mss. nd., MLHM.

4 Much of the preceding paragraphs are based on Kennedy, *The History of Steam Navigation,* pp.21–22, and Jackman, pp.452–6.

5 Jackman, p.455.

6 Garwood, p.7.

7 Kennedy, p.23.

8 Thompson and Yeo, *The Unknown Mayhew,* p.231.

9 op. cit., p.12.

10 Whyman *EKS,* p.58.

11 mss. nd., MLHM.

12 Martin, Evidence to Select Committee on Steam Navigation, p.18.

13 Pimlott, *The Englishman's Holiday,* p.77.

14 Dickens, *Sketches by Boz,* p.128.

15 op. cit., p.272.

16 It may have been a year earlier according to Kennedy, p.30.

17 Report on Steam Vessel Accidents, 1839.

CHAPTER FOUR

CONSEQUENCES: MASS TOURISM

As public confidence grew, the demand for steamboat travel increased so that more of them were brought into service. In 1820 there were thirty-four steamboats registered in Britain; by 1837 there were 531. Because it was easier to apply steam technology to ships, the steamboat was exactly ten years ahead of the steam locomotive railway in development. The speed and amenities of the steamboats were the attraction – they could make several voyages whilst sailing ships were struggling against wind and tide to complete one voyage. By 1822 there was only one passenger hoy left trading from Margate to London. Many switched to carrying bulk freight to Belgian and Dutch ports.

With the steamboat revolution under way, the number of visitors to Margate reached 26,000 in 1818. In that year the first round-trip from London to Margate in a day was achieved. One of the fastest steamers, the *Favorite* (160 tons, and with the *Victory*, built by Evans of Rotherhithe) sailed from London at 4.45 a.m. and reached Margate at 2.00 p.m. She then started the return trip at 2.45p.m. and reached London at 10.00p.m. Information about the weather has not survived, but the fortitude of the 158 passengers was remarkable. The evidence is unclear as to when the first *practicable* return journey *in a day* from London to Margate was possible: it may have been several years later – 1826 or 1827. A report in the *Maidstone Journal* of 26 August 1826 stated that Captain Grant of the *Columbine* (242 tons) had sailed to Margate and back with 660 passengers (presumably from London). But undoubtedly the day trips caught on: an advertisement in *The Times* in June 1829 announced an 'extra-ordinary and interesting marine excursion' to Margate and back, taking '13–14 hours' for 10s. The advertisement said that this was the third annual trip. The vessel was

The *Victory* and *Favorite* at Margate in about 1830, showing the pier and lighthouse. On the nearer vessel the master is perched precariously on the paddle box from where he can give orders. The bridge between paddle boxes was introduced at a later date. In the background are the Georgian terraces of fashionable eighteenth-century Margate. *Commercial postcard by an unknown artist, Margate Local History Museum*

the *Hero*, commanded by Captain Large, and inducements included 'refreshments', and a military band. A brief notice in *The Times* in July 1832 announced a day trip to Ramsgate on the *Harlequin* (250 tons) for less – 6*s* – a venture that must have been largely dependent on good weather for its success.

A passenger enthusiastically described the impression made on him by the facilities on board the *Venus* which he took to Margate, accompanied by an 'agreeable but unfashionable' companion in August 1823:

Embarked at the Tower Stairs…on board the *Venus* Steam Boat for Margate when Boiling & Smoking away at the rate of 12 or 14 miles an hour in the most agreeable stile [sic] to the great delight of nearly 200 cockneys of all ages, sizes & sexes. She (if feminine is the gender of a Steamer) arrived in 7 hours and a half at her destination. The Accommodation of this Vessel is superior to any Sailing Vessel I ever saw. Splendid cabins, Mahogany fittings, Horsehair sofas, Carpetted floors, tiers of Windows like the Ports of a Frigate, with Bars and Bar maids, kitchin [sic] & Cooks, Stewards & Waiters and all the suitable paraphenalia of Splendid Breakfasting & Dinnering Administer their comforts to as easy, lounging genteel and amalgamated a Conglomeration of Passengers as ever promenaded with measured steps to a Band of musicians between the Stem & Stern of a Vessel...[1]

The *Venus* had been launched two years previously and was owned by the Old Margate Co. The speed stated here is on the optimistic side.

The departure of a steamer is described, with some exaggeration, by Dickens:

Then the bell, which is the signal for the Gravesend boat starting, begins to ring most furiously: and people keep time to the bell... The bell stops; the boat starts: people who have been taking leave of their friends on board, are carried away against their will: and people who have been taking leave of their friends on shore, find that they have performed a very needless ceremony, in consequence of their not being carried away at all.[2]

In the year 2005 Gravesend is no longer a resort and seems a sad and neglected place, but in the 1820s the impact of steamer services produced a rapid expansion of leisure and tourist facilities (so that it became a riverside version of Peckham Rye and Hampstead Heath, as J.R. Pimlott says). During this decade 50,000 people visited Gravesend annually, a figure which steadily increased to 120,000 by 1831, and reached nearly 1.5 million *per year* in the mid-1840s. This was mass tourism for the first time in history and the attraction was the seawater, fresh air, and other entertainments – all close to London, which made for cheaper fares and the feasibility of day-trips. The steamboats took about three hours to cover the thirty miles, which was about the same as the coach; if the tide was against the steamboat it would take another half-hour so the coach would be quicker. By 1835 steamboat companies were claiming that Gravesend could be reached from London in two hours – but this was unlikely, and certainly not if the tide was against them. In 1815 the cheaper steamboat fare was 2s but by 1827 competition had reduced it to 1s which was far cheaper than the stagecoach.

The most promising description of Gravesend and its surroundings was in Dickens's *Dictionary of the Thames*:

From the river Gravesend, unlike most riverside towns, presents an attractive appearance. The town rises rapidly from the riverside to the hill which is crowned with the well-known windmill; and the cliffs towards Rosherville and Northfleet, and the well-wooded rising ground towards Chalk and Cobham add greatly to the beauty of the view.[3]

Landing stages, pleasure gardens at nearby Rosherville, Windmill Hill, and hotels, the Clarendon, Roebuck, and Rosherville on the river, baths, and reading rooms were quickly built as it became a popular London resort. Disembarkation during the 1820s was in the hands of the watermen but despite energetic – and understandable – opposition from them, piers were opened: the Town Pier in 1834 (a substantial investment by the corporation: it cost £30,000), Rosherville Pier in 1840, and the Terrace Pier in 1842. Rosherville pleasure gardens, which were the Alton Towers of the nineteenth century, were well-conducted, providing dancing, tea and shrimps, and 'more substantial refreshments'. It was tastefully laid out.

However, whatever the guidebooks said, and of course they only gave good news, *Punch* (a satirical magazine popular with the middle classes) did not take Gravesend very seriously:

> The hotels are numerous and excellent. Like Newgate [prison] each of them professes to be furnished with an *ordinary*. This is a meal at a fixed price, and not a clergyman, as some might suppose, although the name of the Rev. Mr. Carver associates aptly with the object of the announcement. We may add that the meal is well named, as well as the visitors, both being of a very ordinary description.[4]

The demand for the steamboats was such that a new company appeared: the New Steam Packet Co. (later re-named the Star Steam Packet Co.). In the following year it introduced four steamers: *Medway*, *Comet*, *Mercury*, and *Star*. At this time (1834) the last Gravesend sailing ship (they were called *tilt* boats) was withdrawn from passenger service – though fish and other cargoes continued to be carried up to London under sail (presumably the fish was smoked).

On the *Albion* 'a concert, a wonderful illusionist, a ball and an efficient band' were advertised ('efficient' seems to be a commonly used adjective for bands and orchestras at the time). It was possible to buy a penny newspaper – *The Penny Dispatch* – containing stories of romance and murder together with information about hobbies. It was published, together with the other curious material in Holywell Street, off the Strand. Two years later yet another company was formed: the Gravesend Iron Steam Packet Co. which provided services downstream from the Pool – from Hungerford Market Pier (now Charing Cross). Their steamers were named *Father Thames*, *Sons of the Thames*, *Royal Tar*, *Gipsey* and *Rose*. By 1835 there were over 670,000 passengers being carried to Gravesend, which was 60 per cent of the total steamboat traffic from London.[5]

Such was the demand that a year later the Diamond Steam Packet Co. diverted steamboats to the Gravesend service (their ships were named *Diamond*, *Pearl, Gem, Ruby*, and so on). There were now twenty-eight vessels on the London to Gravesend service. Most passengers were day trippers, but for those who were not, Gravesend stands accused of starting the fashion for sleeping on beaches, piers 'or anywhere else'.[6] The appeal of Gravesend – especially Rosherville – had widened and it was no longer middle class. Some services called at Brunswick Wharf at Blackwall (opened as a steam wharf in 1835 by the East India Dock Co.), which took forty-five minutes to an hour to reach. In order to speed up the journey from the City to Blackwall a railway was opened in July 1840; such was the popularity of this that, in 1844, two-thirds of passengers landing and embarking at Gravesend had used the Blackwall railway.

Although blighted by a reputation in some quarters for being unhealthy, Southend had been fashionable for a short time. Steamboat services from London increased steadily: in 1826 there were three per week, provided by *Sir Joseph Yorke*; in 1832 there were six per week, and *William IV* had been added to the fleet. In 1838 services were daily with the service having been augmented by the *Duke of Sussex*, *Prince George*, *Rose*, *Hawk* of the Commercial Co. But the railway from Fenchurch Street arrived in 1856 and steadily drew off traffic from the steamboats.

Further along the Thames estuary, Herne Bay was planned as a seaside resort of the steamboat era:

> Early in the year 1830, two capitalists…drove to Herne Bay… They were soon struck with the unwrought condition, and the death-like inactivity of everything around them… A project of magnitude was formed. It was nothing less than erecting a pier, to enable passengers and goods to be landed at all times of the tide…and a committee of the principal landowners and others was appointed when they drew up a plan for forming a company… The plans were drawn up by the late Mr [Thomas] Telford, whose abilities as a skilful engineer are well known.[7]

The speculators invested £50,000 in the construction of a pier, which opened in 1832. It was over half a mile (1,000 yards) long, and a narrow-gauge railway was installed which was intended for luggage, but precariously carried passengers. Propulsion was by wind if available, otherwise by hand. A statue of William IV had been intended for the entrance but was never built. The pier lasted for thirty years until it was attacked by teredo worms and closed in 1864. A replacement was opened in 1873 but was shorter and could not be used at low tide and by this time most visitors were arriving by train. The town of Herne Bay was laid out with a promenade (about a mile long), streets, and a hotel. From here coaches ran to Canterbury and to Dover. The town and its amenities must have provided employment for local people. A company was formed – the Herne Bay Steam Packet Co., which provided two elegant and popular steamers, the *Red Rover* and, appropriately, *City of Canterbury*. The number of passengers to Herne Bay increased from 31,000 in 1838 to nearly

40,000 in 1842. Allowance needs to be made for the fact that 1838 was a wet summer, but it was nevertheless an impressive achievement.

And, of course, Margate prospered from the wave of mass tourism. *Punch* said:

> We have sometimes thought Margate not unlike Tottenham Court Road broken into streets, and removed to the seaside for the benefit of the sea air. Ramsgate gives one the idea of Pentonville introduced to the ocean for a similar advantage.[8]

And in respect of the latter resort, Dickens describes a merry scene:

> ...the *City of London* Ramsgate steamer was running gaily down the river. Her flag was flying, her band was playing, her passengers were conversing; every thing about her seemed gay and lively...[9]

Between 1817 and 1835 steamboat traffic to Margate quadrupled: in the former year there had been 26,000 visitors, when the voyage took six to seven hours, by the latter year there were 108,000 passengers arriving after a voyage of five hours. By 1846 it was claimed that the journey was down to four and three-quarter hours. Scepticism about these claims is entirely justified – much must have depended on tides and weather.

In 1820, five steamers were running from London to Margate; by 1827 this had exactly doubled – six belonging to Brocklebank's 'Old' Margate company, and four to the General Steam Navigation Co. (GSNC). In Appendix B there is more information on this company – it was important in the history of the steamboat, because of its size and the fact that it was adequately capitalised (unlike many other owners).

In the 1820s the total number of passengers exceeded half a million; in 1841–42 alone, 96,777 passengers landed and embarked at Margate, which was a slight reduction from another good year – 1835. Due to the buoyant demand, a new company was formed at Margate – the Margate and London 'New Co.' – with the *Royal George* and the *Essex*. Traffic increased with fare reductions of up to 50 per cent, requiring more frequent services which were provided by six operators in the late 1830s and early 1840s. Regrettably, the fortunes of the Margate companies are not well documented, although it is on record that one of their steamers, the *Magnet,* collided with the *Red Rover* of the Herne Bay Co. in 1836. Little is known of them after that. In the mid-1830s a guide was published in London (it was undated) called *A New Steam-Boat Companion*. Predictably, this was full of exaggeration, most of it pardonable given that it was intended to boost traffic. Here is a sample of what the reader would be treated to:

…such is the wonderful state of perfection to which steam has been bought, that a passage by water is quite as certain and regular, as a journey by land in a stage-coach. Nor can it fail to be a source of the greatest astonishment to those persons who have not been accustomed to steam vessels, when they find the accommodation on board so convenient…refreshments may be procured on board of the best quality, at moderate charges.[10]

As already mentioned something quite new was provided: hot, cooked, meals whilst actually travelling/moving, i.e. without having to stop for them, as had been the practice with stagecoaches, and as would be the practice on the railways until the introduction of restaurant cars:

It would be an act of injustice to the stewards, were we not to notice their great activity and civility, and the excellence of the refreshments provided. The dinner which consists of joints, boiled and roasted, of the very best quality; all vegetables that are in season; and pastry wines and dessert etc is served up in a style both pleasing and surprising when the size of the kitchen is considered.[11]

The impact of the steamer on Margate and Ramsgate was therefore considerable – especially on the former, which initially had no pier: at low tide passengers were landed from small boats and precariously carried over the rocks by the porters (one hopes that in carrying young ladies first, the porters did not keep their mothers waiting too long). The harbour wall, called the pier, was designed by John Rennie in 1815 for the steamer service, but could only be used at high tide. It curved to the west with a lighthouse at the end.

As services increased a second pier was opened in 1824. This protruded from the base of Rennie's stone pier – where it joined the esplanade, and was a wooden structure of fifty yards extending north into deep water so that it could be used at low tide. The jetty was named after the chairman of the Pier & Harbour Co., Dr Daniel Jarvis, and it meant that arrangements were better than those at the Pool of London in that passengers could disembark from ship to shore at all tides without the use of small boats. Instead of a royal statue it had a 'handsome and richly ornamented cast-iron archway' at the entrance which was put up in tribute to Dr Jarvis.[12] The hub of the two piers was a meeting place and focal point in Margate.

Although John Ruskin arrogantly called Margate 'one of the most prosaic of English watering places', and that great radical, William Cobbett, dismissed it as a settlement of 'stockjobbing cuckolds',[13] it unquestionably provided pleasure for many hard-pressed Londoners, despite the middle-class intellectuals. It has been asserted, possibly correctly, that the steamboats crowded out the aristocracy and the gentry.[14] *The Times* said in 1824 that the steamboats were giving the Kent coast a 'prodigous lift', but lamented (as it would)

The lighthouse at Margate – an engraving by an unknown artist of three steamboats, creating a lot of wash and commotion at a crowded pier. *Author's collection*

the absence of the aristocracy and the 'leading nobility' of Kent. Instead the visitors came from what it called eastern London – but were not proletarian: they were richer merchants, East India directors and bankers. *Punch* had a dig at them by calling them 'seasick cockney emigrants'. Each boat would be met by a horde of cab-drivers, hoteliers, innkeepers, and boarding housekeepers.

There is a delightful description of the arrival of a steamboat at Margate from a contemporary novel which is worth quoting at length. In a hot London summer in the 1830s, R.S. Surtees' hapless hero, Mr Jorrocks, a 'heavenly simpleton', decides to escape the 'ungrateful hurry of the town' by spending a few days in Margate. He takes with him two friends:

At the wharf below the (London) Bridge there lay a magnificent steamer, painted pea-green and white, with flags flying from her masts, and the deck swarming with smart bonnets and bodices. Her name was the *Royal Adelaide*...

It was nearly eight o'clock ere the *Royal Adelaide* touched the point of the far-famed Margate Jetty, a fact that was announced as well by the usual bump, and scuttle to the side to get out first, as

The *Royal Adelaide*, employed on service between London, Gravesend and Margate. She was typical of the many paddle steamers to be seen on the London river in the early 1880s.

by the band striking up *God Save The King*, and the mate demanding the tickets of the passengers.

Two or three other cargoes of cockneys having arrived before, the whole place was in commotion, and the beach swarmed with spectators as anxious to watch this last disembarkation as they had been to see the first. By a salutary regulation of the sages who watch over the interests of the town, 'all manner of persons' are prohibited from walking on the jetty during this ceremony, but the platform of which it is composed being very low, those who stand upon the beach outside the rails, are just about on a right level to shoot their impudence cleverly into the ears of the newcomers who are paraded along two lines of gaping, quizzing, jeering citizens, who fire volleys of wit and satire upon them as they pass... When they got to the gate at the end, the tide of fashion became obstructed by the kissings of husbands and wives, the greetings of fathers and sons, the officiousness of porters, the cries of flymen, the importunities of innkeepers, the cards of bathing-women, the salutations of donkey-drivers...mingled in one common flood of indescribable confusion. [15]

There are drawings of Margate by J.M.W. Turner from about 1786, according to his recent biographer, James Hamilton. It is possible that Turner was sent to school there. In any event,

Margate gets a kind word from Hamilton, according to whom it was, in the 1820s and 1830s, 'the neatest, cleanest, brightest, most invigorating and entertaining seaside town of them all'.[16] Visitors were attracted 'by the entertainments, the architecture and the society of the town, and also by the claim that the sea water and air could cure all ills'. Turner knew the 'elegant Georgian squares, terraces, the theatres, music and society. He knew the bathing machines in the bay'.[17] Turner was fascinated, Hamilton says, by the extremes of weather and in capturing the power of the sea. The painting *Sunrise with Sea Monsters* possibly depicts a steamer being devoured by a huge fish, whilst *Rockets and Blue Lights* brings nature and technology together – the rough sea will swamp the steamers which are being warned?

Hamilton recounts how, in the summer of 1838, Turner left London to stay with his friend, Mrs Booth, in Margate. Hamilton quotes the ballad 'The Margate Voyage', which, he says, 'captures the thrill of departure in the steamboat *Adelaide*':

Off we went with our tall chimney smoking,

Five hundred, all squeezing and choking;

Some their heads o'er the vessel's side poking,

Which made their gay spirits much tamer.

But John Bull, though ever so cross, sir,

Is never at meals at a loss, sir;

So they soon began beef-steaks to toss, sir;

Down their throats in the *Adelaide* steamer. [18]

Turner could observe the sea at fairly close quarters, as well as the sky, in the midst of its vastness, though the crush of passengers (according to Hamilton) would not allow him to do much more than make cursory sketches:

Most of the time he hung over the stern, watching the effects of the sun and the boiling foam. About two o'clock he would open his wallet of cold meat in the cabin, and, nearing himself to one with whom he was in the habit of chatting, would beg a clean plate and a hot potato, and did not refuse one glass of wine, but would never accept two. It need hardly be added that he was no favourite with the waiters.[19]

Turner used the steamboats to roam up and down the coast – Broadstairs, Ramsgate, Deal and Dover. In Hamilton's opinion, Turner's *Sunrise with Sea Monsters* can also be taken to be Jarvis's landing place at Margate.[20]

A steamboat's arrival at Ramsgate is vividly described by Dickens:

> The sun was shining brightly; the sea, dancing to its own music, rolled merrily in; crowds of people
> promenaded to and fro, young ladies tittered, old ladies talked, nursemaids displayed their charms
> to the greatest possible advantage, and their sweet little charges ran up and down, and to and fro,
> and in and out, under the feet, and between the legs of the assembled concourse, in the most
> playful and exhilirating manner possible. There were old gentlemen trying to make out objects
> through long telescopes, and young ones making objects of themselves in open shirt-collars; ladies
> carrying about portable chairs, and portable chairs carrying about invalids; parties waiting on the
> peer [sic] for parties who had come by the steam-boat.[21]

Leisure and entertainment in these two resorts expanded to meet demand. The Theatre
Royal (where Dora Jordan, the greatest comic actress of the age, made her last appearance),
the Assembly Rooms, and the Tivoli Gardens flourished at Margate. *Punch* commented on
the proliferation of boarding houses, and actually praised the theatre. Margate goes down
in history for pioneering popular amusements: a *camera obscura*, donkey rides, sporting
contests on the sands, and – to accomodate the changeable climate – indoor attractions such
as auctions, dice, lotteries, raffles, and bazaars (hence Ruskin's disapproval).[22] Ultimately,
to the wage-earning excursionist Margate offered 'fresh air, shrimps, winkles, and whelks,
all washed down with plenty of beer'. [23]

 Whereas Margate attracted all social classes, Ramsgate was regarded by *Punch* as quieter
and more select:

> The folks who congregate at Margate appear to have only six days to cleanse their animal spirits
> from the dust and cobwebs that for the previous three hundred and fifty nine have hung about and
> clogged them at their desks and counters; whilst the visitors of Ramsgate, in lieu of six days allow
> them at least a fortnight. Hence they take pleasure with a certain calmness… The amusements of
> Ramsgate are few and innocent. A frolic over a pint of shrimps at Pegwell Bay, or a rush to take a
> lounge at St Lawrence is, perhaps, the wildest outburst allowed to metropolitan dissipation.[24]

As Ramsgate was considered socially superior to Gravesend and Margate, it was chosen for a
holiday by Dickens' fictional family of social climbers, the Tuggs in *Sketches by Boz*. It was also
chosen by the artist W.P. Frith for his painting *Ramsgate Sands* when he became bored with
costume painting. For the local people, employment opportunities improved: in addition to
hotels, boarding houses, and restaurants, the steamers had to be supplied with coal and provisions. Water was supplied by pumps adjacent to the harbour, and coal was stored on the pier.
The provision of coal was a labour-intensive operation. Steamers on the Gravesend service used
three tons of coal per day, so it would have been at least double this for the Ramsgate run.

NOTES

1 'Early Steamboat Travelling: A voyage to Margate in 1823'. Cutting from an unknown newspaper dated 2 February 1895.

2 Dickens, p.127.

3 Op. cit., p.79.

4 Op. cit., p.49.

5 Cunningham, *Leisure in the Industrial Revolution* p.160. From the 1840s *Jupiter, Mars,* and *Venus,* owned by the Star Co., were sailing from Blackwall to Gravesend, together with three iron steamboats, *Railway: Brunswick,* and *Blackwall.* These last three, which were rather unimaginatively named, belonged to the Blackwall railway which opened in 1840. Such was the demand that two other steamboats transferred from the Pool to Blackwall: *Father Thames* and *Sons of The Thames.*

6 Walton, p.18.

7 Whyman, *EKS*, p.84.

8 *Punch,* collected ed July–December 1842 p.48.

9 Dickens, p.391.

10 Op cit, p.3.

11 Whyman, *EKS*, p.68.

12 Op cit, p.86.

13 Pimlott, p.162.

14 Walton, p.18.

15 R.S. Surtees *Mr Jorrocks Jaunts and Jollities* 1971 edn, p.129.

16 Hamilton, p.244.

17 *Ibid.*

18 Op. cit., p.280 qu. AGH Bacharach *Turner's Holland,* 1994.

19 Op. cit. p.281 qu. Alaric Watts 'Biographical Sketch of J.M.W.T.' *Liber Fluviorum,* 1853 xxxii.

20 *Ibid.*

21 Dickens, p.394.

22 Margate Charter Trustees nd, *Margate: A Resort History.*

23 Twyman mss, p.27.

24 *Punch,* p.45 and p.49.

CHAPTER FIVE

TAKING THE STEAMER TO WORK

PREVIEW

For the British Isles, coastal shipping had always been an important form of transport, and from around 1820 there was a rapid expansion in the number of steamboats trading from the major ports in the North. Services from Liverpool to Belfast and from Liverpool to Glasgow were started in the summer of that year. The latter was expected to perform the journey in about thirty hours. A Liverpool to Dublin service was introduced (more of this shortly). In the spring of 1821 a new steamboat, the *Soho,* was launched on the river Tay at Perth. She was the largest so far and was placed on the Edinburgh to London service. Two large steamboats of over 400 tons, with engines of 100hp, the *City of Edinburgh* and *James Watt* were also introduced to this service; they did not carry cargo, and amazingly had sleeping accommodation for 100 passengers. In the following year, 1822, the Plymouth, Devonport, Portsmouth & Falmouth Steam Packet Co. was formed, providing regular services to each of these ports. The port of Hull was a major player and by 1826 there were twenty-six steamships operating with London as their southern limit. Expansion continued and nine years later the number had increased to about forty, some of which were trading to Holland. By 1836 there was one owner operating seven vessels and one operating eight vessels between Plymouth and London. Regularity and reliability in comparison to sailing vessels were the attraction. Moreover they were a cheaper and safer mode of travel than the stagecoach. They carried mail. But the weather could be a deterrent and passenger services fluctuated according to seasonal demand. Regrettably many of them are not documented.

The East Coast

By 1830 services from London to Leith (the port for Edinburgh) sailed from the lower Thames – those of GSNC from Greenwich, and the rivals, the London & Edinburgh, from the Brunswick Steam Wharf at Blackwall (ten years before the railway arrived there). Demand was such that in 1831 another company – the London Leith Edinburgh & Glasgow Shipping Co., one of the earliest having operated sailing vessels since 1814 – introduced three steamboats. Later, competition was reduced when the London & Edinburgh was taken over by GSNC in 1836. In the next decade GSNC's advertised service comprised the *Clarence* sailing from Leith to London on Saturday afternoons; in the evening of the same day a vessel did the reverse trip from London – probably the *Leith*, which had joined that route. In 1844 the *Royal William* (307 tons) and the *Royal Adelaide* of the London Leith Co. were sailing to and from St Katharine's Wharf to Leith and back on Wednesdays and Saturdays. London to Scotland was an important market for the coastal trade but pooling agreements between the ship owners restricted competition.[1]

The Aberdeen & London Shipping Co. and the Aberdeen & London Steam Navigation Co., competitors in the coastal trade, amalgamated in November 1835 and formed the Aberdeen Steam Navigation Co. They owned three steamships, and provided a weekly service to London; four years later the company merged with the Hull Shipping Co. and gained a monopoly on the Hull–Aberdeen route. By 1844 they had expanded and were employing five vessels, and now traded to Hull as well as London. After some hesitation they expanded further and bought the steamer *North Star* which sailed to and from Inverness. One of their vessels was the *Queen of Scotland* (claimed to be nearly 1,000 tons) and the *Duke of Wellington* (335 tons). They sailed from the Aberdeen Steam Wharf which was between London Bridge Wharf and Custom House. An important cargo was live cattle, sheep, and pigs for the London meat markets. In 1836 7,000 head of cattle and 10,000 sheep were brought to London. Some steamers did not carry merely light, high-value goods and perishables, but whatever could be taken, including timber, cast iron, oil, cotton yarn and waste, salmon, and occasionally detachments of garrison troops.

In the mid-1840s there were two ships running to Dundee, from Hore's Steam Wharf at Wapping where passengers could dodge the watermen and 'walk on board without the inconvenience of boats'. Later the service to Newcastle sailed from this wharf. Dundee and Perth had been linked to London by steamboat since 1824. A firm called Martin & Burns started a London–Dundee service in 1832 with two vessels (the names are not known), as a result of which the Dundee Perth & London Shipping Co. ordered two vessels which

Three steamboats of the General Steam Navigation Co. off Brunswick Wharf in the early 1840s, after the opening of the London & Blackwall Railway. The *Clarence*, 800 tons, is sailing for Leith, the *Leith*, 494 tons, is arriving from Leith, and the *Columbine*, 242 tons, is arriving from Rotterdam. *National Maritime Museum, PY8846*

The *Royal William* in a strong following wind, crowded with passengers. This picture is dated from 1840, when this steamboat was owned by the New Margate Co.: she was acquired by General Steam Navigation in 1849. *Author's collection*

started trading in 1834: the *Dundee* and the *Perth*. Interestingly, Frank Burtt's *Cross Channel and Coastal Paddle Steamers* contains an extract from the log of the *Dundee* which shows her sailing from Dundee on 2 April 1834 at 9.12 a.m. and reaching her moorings in London at 10.30 a.m. on 4 April. She had anchored for the night of the 3 April somewhere north of the Nore. This was a pretty good voyage but the Dundee steamers were laid up in winter, and trade was resumed by sailing vessels, which slowed the journey somewhat.

By the mid-1830s navigational aids in the form of lights and buoys were introduced on the East Coast[2] though major accidents still happened; Frank Burtt refers to the *Forfarshire* which was wrecked on the Farne Islands off the Northumberland coast on 7 September 1838. This tragedy has passed into legend because the daughter of the Longstone Lighthouse keeper, Grace Darling, helped rescue survivors. In the late 1830s GSNC experimented with services to Berwick (where a local company put on a steamboat to compete with them), Sunderland, and Ipswich. A company appeared in Sunderland in the 1840s when GSNC had withdrawn. The new mode of steam transport was full of incident. The *Kingston* sailed for London at 4.00 p.m. on 28 April 1821 with forty passengers and cargo. Four hours later she broke down and returned under sail, taking thirty-six hours to cover what had taken four hours under steam – a good illustration of the comparative speeds of steam and sail. After repairs she sailed on 12 May and did 260 miles in thirty-five hours at 7.4 knots. She was followed by the *Yorkshireman*, and then the *Prince Frederick*. These three vessels were owned by a locally financed firm called the Hull Steamboat Packet Co. which had a monopoly on the London trade for twelve years.

The *London* followed in 1827 and expansion continued with the *Albatross* in 1834 and the *William Darley* in the following year. With this level of demand it was inevitable that a rival company would be formed, and the Humber Union Steamship Co. introduced the *Enterprise* in 1833 followed by the *City of Glasgow* three years later. This vessel was financed by Robert Pearson of Stanton's Wharf, London, and two Hull businessmen.

The Humber Union then ordered two vessels from the Limehouse yard of Curling & Young which were launched within three weeks of each other in 1836: *Vivid* and *Waterwitch* (276 tons). The former made the passage to London in twenty-three hours in 1836. The latter reached the pinnacle of respectability by carrying the Dean of York to London, accompanied by 200 passengers. This company was hoping for a more upper-class market – in the way that the airlines covet the first- and business-class passenger today: their advertisements were aimed at 'noblemen and gentlemen travelling with their suites' and went on to claim that 'passengers will be conveyed with all the comfort of a first-rate Inn at a greater speed than by coach, and often superior to that of the mails, at less than half the expense'.[3] In fact there had been problems: a new owner introduced the *City of Glasgow* with higher fares,

A Collier off Greenwich. Colliers were not popular with steamboat captains, or any other mariners – the sheer number of them in the Thames made navigation hazardous. This fine pen and ink drawing is dated from 1829 but the artist is not knwon. *Greenwich Libraries*

1842 THE DOCKYARD AT WOOLWICH.

Woolwich – the destination of many local steamboats. The Royal Dockyard closed in 1869. From here the ferry across the river to North Woolwich has operated since 1889. *Greenwich Libraries*

of 10s first and 5s second class but the attraction was that the voyage would be 'free from the danger of pickpockets and overcrowding…in compliance with the recommendation of a number of friends, who prefer paying a reasonable fare to the danger and discomfort of overcrowding at very low fares'.[4] This ship also had wash basins in the cabins. The elegant and lengthy *Wilberforce* followed in June 1837, which was also built by Curling & Young. She was 179ft long and the largest steamboat yet built for Hull owners. They traded to St Katharine's Wharf.

In the face of this competition Hull steamboats reduced their fares to 4s first class and 2s second class with an average passage of twenty-six hours, and introduced the *Victoria*. She was large (1,200 tons), her engines were designed by David Napier, the renowned Scottish engineer, and she sailed from the Humber in March 1838, but on a disastrous voyage. On reaching the Thames her boiler flue collapsed and six of the engine room crew were killed. Three months later, in June 1838, her boiler exploded, killing nine persons, most probably members of the crew. These accidents have been attributed to her racing the *Wilberforce*.[5] In this case, competition proved not only destructive in terms of loss of life, but commercially destructive: the Humber Union was forced out of business by price-cutting, and their vessels – the *Wilberforce*, *Vivid*, and *Waterwitch* – were sold to GSNC in 1841.

In the 1830s the Norfolk Steam Packet Co. operated the *Ailsa Craig* (171 tons) from London to Great Yarmouth – the advertisements stated Great Yarmouth *and* Norwich but there is no evidence as to whether or not there was sufficient draught for a steamer to sail up the Yare. A service to Great Yarmouth had started as early as 1819.

GSNC advertised fares in May 1844 at 17s 6d for the best cabin from Hull to London (horses were £2 2s), less to Great Yarmouth at 15s (with horses at £1 1s), and predictably, higher to Newcastle at £1 10s, and Edinburgh at £3 10s (with horses at £5 5s) It is not known how many passengers took their equine companions with them, but it certainly increased the cost of travel. The stagecoach fares were higher: for example £3 5s inside and £1 14s outside was charged from London to Hull. Many coaches were taken off in the summer months, but the steamboats, like the railways later, produced feeder traffic – from the ports to inland towns. There was a general reduction in fares on the East Coast trade in 1845 – there had been a recession in the early 1840s, then a revival in 1846–47, and then a downturn again caused by the political instability on the Continent – revolutions in Germany and France in 1848. The year of the Great Exhibition, 1851, was a good year, when steamers brought visitors from the East Coast to London.

The cargo trade from Hull was, as with many East Coast ports, dead meat, and also high-value manufactured goods from Leeds, Sheffield, as well as Hull itself. A commodity such as cutlery from Sheffield may well have been an example of a high-value cargo.

The state of play with the East Coast trade by 1839 was as follows: there were passenger services from London to Yarmouth, Hull, Goole, Scarborough, Whitby, Stockton-on-Tees, Newcastle, Berwick, Edinburgh, Dundee, Perth, and Aberdeen. There was no direct service to Inverness, but a steamer ran from Edinburgh.[6]

THE IRISH SEA

A steamboat service was started across the Mersey from Liverpool to Eastham (Cheshire) in 1816 at a return fare of 1s (which was not cheap): it connected with coaches to and from Chester, Shrewsbury, and Holyhead. In the same year a service from Holyhead to Dublin was started with the steamer *Hibernia* which crossed the Irish Sea in seven hours. Thomas Telford built a good road to Holyhead and the railway opened in 1850. This service across the Irish Sea has lasted to the present time.

Services from London to Dublin were inaugurated in 1826. Steam propulsion revolutionised shipping in the Irish Sea; from 1824 twelve steamboats were trading between Liverpool, Dublin, and Belfast. What must have been the longest coastal voyage was from London to Glasgow; this was on the *Erin* and was advertised as putting into Plymouth, Dublin and Belfast, but it may have called also at Falmouth and probably Swansea, for coal and water. From 1831 to 1835, the *William Fawcett* of 206 tons, built by Caleb Smith of Liverpool in 1829, was trading between London and Dublin for the London Steam Packet Co. There is a model of her in Southampton Maritime Museum from where she sailed for the Peninsular Steam Co. and ran to Spain and Portugal. By 1839 steamship services from London to Dublin, and to Liverpool, had ceased, doubtless because London and Liverpool were connected by railway in 1838.[7]

An Irish undertaking, the St George's Steam Packet Co., provided services to Ireland and West Country ports. By 1836 it had twenty vessels operating from its London wharf. This company was exceptional, because like GSN, it had more than one route, unlike the majority of companies and individual owners who were based on a single port. For example, the *Zephyr* sailed for Exeter, Torquay, and the Channel Islands. This vessel did not have a wharf: embarkation was in mid-stream in the care of the watermen at St Katharine's Stairs and Alderman's Stairs.

The British & Irish Steamship Co. advertised what was called, in the vernacular of the time, 'steam intercourse – twice a week' for a service between London and Liverpool, calling at Plymouth, Falmouth, and Dublin (it may well have called at Swansea for coal and water). Some of the ships carried passengers and the emphasis on steam stressed its reliability in comparison to sail. On some services a disclaimer announced that a pilot might

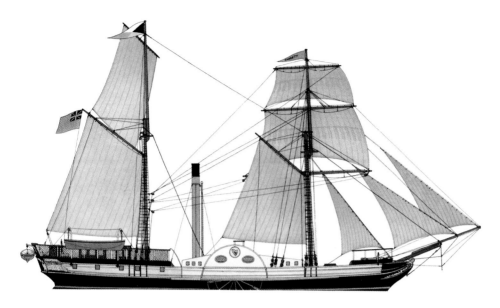

The *William Fawcett*, 206 tons. Built by Caleb Smith of Liverpool in 1829, with an engine of 160 hp. She traded between London and Dublin for the London Steam Packet Co. from 1831 to 1835. She was later sold to the Peninsular Steam Co. (forerunner of P&O) and opened a mail service from Southampton to Spain and Portugal from 1840. *Author's collection.*

The *William Fawcett*, the first P&O steam ship.

or might not be employed when leaving port (ships, except for the mail steamers, were supposed to take pilots in and out of Liverpool by Act of Parliament) and that the ship had 'liberty to tow', i.e. was likely to tow a sailing ship on the way out to sea – a profitable undertaking for the steamers.[8] Away from London there were regular services from, for example, Hull to Dundee and Liverpool to Glasgow. The City of Dublin Steam Packet Co. ran a service from Belfast and Dublin to Le Havre with a steamship called *Thames*.[9]

THE CHANNEL

The map and guide published by Moggs in 1839 shows services from London to Dover, Portsmouth, Southampton (this would not have lasted much longer because the railway opened to Southampton in the following year), Torquay, and Dartmouth. No direct service is shown to either Plymouth or Falmouth, but there was a service from Portsmouth to Plymouth (and a service from Exeter to Plymouth). It is surprising that there was no service to Falmouth, given that there was no railway to what was an important port.[10]

NOTES

1 Palmer *Thesis,* p.158.

2 John Shelley, evidence in *Report on Manufacturing*, q.7991, p.492.

3 Pearson, p.80.

4 Op. cit., p.31.

5 Arthur G Credland. *John Ward of Hull* nd on which information about Hull is based.

6 *Moggs Map of Steam Navigation,* 1839.

7 *Ibid.*

8 *Manchester Guardian,* 1 December 1838.

9 Op. cit. 7 July 1838

10 *Moggs Map of Steam Navigation,* 1 Jan 1839.

CHAPTER SIX

PASSENGERS

It is the hottest long vacation known for many years. All the young clerks are madly in love, and, according to their various degrees, pine for bliss with the beloved object, at Margate, Ramsgate, or Gravesend.[1]

Transport history is often social history, and one of the most important aspects of this story is the users of the steamboats – the passengers. Who were they and who benefited from the introduction of steam technology?

To look at this in more detail is speculative but rewarding. Ship passenger lists were not required until the 1870s – beyond the steamboat era – and would not have been compiled for excursions to the north Kent coastal resorts, nor for the coastal services to the East Coast and Scotland. Some sort of record may have been compiled for Continental services; passengers were required to obtain passports for the country of destination from consular offices in Britain until 1861, but little documentation has survived.

TOURISTS

It is reasonable to suppose that in the early years of the steamboats the young clerks in *Bleak House*, from where the above quotation comes, would not have been able to afford the fares. Their salaries were in the region of £100 to £130 per year, i.e. from £2 to £2 10s per week.[2] The lowest fares to Margate were 12s in the 1820s, which came down to 10s in the last part of the decade, and then 6s from 1835 onwards. At periods of intense competition in the 1830s the fares were lower – the Commercial Steam Packet Co. only charged 3s on Mondays, Wednesdays, and Fridays in July 1835[3] – though few clerks would have been able to get away from their counting houses and offices on a weekday. Gravesend was a better bet for the young clerks: fares were in the region of 2s, as already mentioned.

Therefore, up to the end of the 1820s, the passengers would have been from the upper class and the middling sort of people – the growing London professional classes, such as lawyers, doctors, and engineers. There would also have been naval and military officers, together with the commercial classes of stock-jobbers, brokers, tradesmen, shopkeepers, mechanics and skilled artisans – all with their wives, daughters, sisters, cousins, and female friends.

Some passengers would have been from the rentier class – of independent means living on a variety of investments especially gilts – the 'funds'. *Bleak House* is set in the early 1830s, by which time the fares had come down to make the steamboats available to shopkeepers, small traders, artisans, and many people in regular employment. By 1845 trips to Gravesend had come down to 9d return, which would certainly have appealed to a mass market.

Gravesend (and Greenwich) would have been especially attractive, as cheap day excursion-fares would have been on offer, as already mentioned. On summer Sunday mornings three steamers would arrive early at Gravesend, whose passengers – probably 1,000 in total – were described as artisans and mechanics, who were to be found 'spreading their little cloths, and taking their refreshment on the grass' – they were family groups on a family outing.[4] But those on the lowest rungs of the social ladder, the unskilled labourers, who were numerous enough, but with only casual employment, had difficulty in affording these fares.

The cut-price day excursion fares which allowed a broad swathe of working people to use the steamboats were not liked by sections of the (middle-class) press. It was reported by some journalists that 'respectable' passengers were annoyed by them and were afraid of 'moral contamination'. The steamboat owners probably made a useful profit from the sale of alcohol, and the drinking and boisterous behaviour offended other passengers. Certainly pickpockets and thieves had rich pickings.

The solicitor to the Star Steam Packet Co. of Gravesend said that the town received one million visitors annually, most of whom were of the 'mercantile' class and came from the City and its immediate environs, which he said included Whitechapel and Lambeth.[5] The City had a residential population of 150,000 up to the mid-century and, as the Gravesend solicitor said, many passengers would have also come from the surrounding districts, such as Shoreditch, Spitalfields, Hackney, Camberwell (noted as a respectable suburb with a growing number of clerks, though for Dickens the 'shabby-genteel' districts of Somers and Camden Towns, Islington, and Pentonville, were where the 'clerk population' lived), Bermondsey, and Southwark. These latter two have been described as 'ancient industrial centres'.[6]

On the riverside there were warehouses for timber, sugar, tobacco, rum and molasses. Colonial expansion in the eighteenth century had brought economic growth so that there had been an expansion in skilled trades such as machine and toolmakers, carriage-makers, coopers, rope makers and carpenters, and the formation of a new and distinctive class of shop-keepers, stallholders, and small traders. These serviced the middle-class families in banking, insurance, and administration – as Roy Porter has said: 'London's high wage economy sucked in thousands creating further spirals of demand'.[7] There was a rapid expansion of industry in the East End and by 1840 most of the crowded frontage of the river was occupied. Up to the mid-century there were prosperous shipyards at Limehouse, Blackwall, Millwall, and Rotherhithe, as well as engineering companies such as Maudslay at Lambeth.

Alarmingly, the day excursions led to overcrowding, as *The Times* noted on 23 May 1839:

> The manner in which the steamers are crammed with passengers during the holy days is highly
> dangerous… The little boats carried 300, 400, and 500 persons and the larger ones…to
> Gravesend, Herne Bay, and Margate frequently took down and brought up 500, 1,000, and 1,500
> passengers. Collisions were nearly occurring several times between the rival steamers…[and]…it
> is fearful to contemplate the dreadful sacrifice of human life which must have been the result if a
> collision had taken place.

Although many people were used to walking to their destinations, they may well, in holiday mood, have treated their families to a cab to reach whichever wharf they were embarking from; the middle classes would certainly have arrived in cabs and carriages, which is confirmed by Dickens (see later). The cabs were not cheap: the return fare from Islington to London Bridge Wharf was about 2s 6d.

Of course the Sabbatarians were alarmed by the travelling and recreation on Sundays, and the issue was considered by the House of Commons Select Committee on the Observance of the Sabbath Day in 1832 – one witness complained that Gravesend resembled a fair on Sundays and that the tranquillity of the town was disturbed. But the money made from the excursionist by the local tradesmen far outweighed the theological considerations. It was pointed out that many people were working during the week, including Saturdays, and that the leisured classes 'go down in the week time'.[8] Furthermore, witnesses emphasised the decorous behaviour of the (working-class) excursionists at Gravesend, and described passengers on a Margate steamer reading religious books (on a Sunday).

For obvious reasons, Sunday travelling thrived – in the mid-1830s the steamers were landing over 8,000 people at Gravesend on the Sabbath. Travel on this day was to become a

SEVENTH EDITION.

THE

GRAVESEND GUIDE,

ADAPTED

TO THE USE OF THE

VISITORS & INHABITANTS,

CONTAINING

MUCH USEFUL AND AMUSING INFORMATION.

To which is added the

Steam-Boat Companion

To Gravesend.

EMBELLISHED WITH AN ACCURATE VIEW OF THE

GRAVESEND BATHING ESTABLISHMENT.

BY JOHN EDWARD HOBCRAFT.

London:

PRINTED AND PUBLISHED BY

WILLIAM MASON, 21, CLERKENWELL GREEN

Sold also by the Author, 9, Princes Street, Gravesend,

AND BY ALL BOOKSELLERS.

PRICE SIXPENCE.

1830.

Left: The Gravesend Guide and the *Steam-Boat Companion* – the cover of an 1830 guide to Gravesend, when this resort was approaching the height of its popularity. It contains timetables and information about the steamboats. *Gravesend Library*

Below: This 1828 engraving of Gravesend shows a variety of craft, with a steamboat in the middle: the *Hawk*, built in 1826. *London's Transport Museum, 3052-32*

bone of contention for the railways, whose timetables avoided the hours of divine worship. Further evidence about passengers comes from the 1841 census, in which occupations were identified. So far as *resident* holiday-making was concerned, Margate was a middle-class resort with over 1,200 resident visitors who were in lodgings, boarding houses, and hotels. Of these, 352 were of independent means with eighty nine servants and governesses. Of the 352 of independent means, 222 were women, some of whom had husbands left behind in London. Of the male visitors, 130 were of independent means, seventy were trades people, thirty-two were merchants, and twenty-seven were drawn from the professions. The last three figures seem to include mechanics, engineers, and clerks. There were only three titled visitors, and farming and the church were numerically insignificant, that is to say there were few of them. What this shows is that Margate had moved from being an upper-class and upper-middle-class-resort to a resort for very much middling people; the upper strata of society now frowned on it, and if they did continue to patronise Margate and Ramsgate they would go late in the season. Nevertheless, the *Morning Herald* was able to report in July 1827 that one grandee, the Duke of Devonshire, travelled to Margate and back by steamer. He made himself popular for he 'caused his own fruit to be produced at the dessert, and permitted his servants to wait upon the company at table'.[9]

The origin of the visitors is not given but it is safe to assume that most were Londoners. A contemporaneous account confirms this:

> ...at the height of the season...[the number of visitors]...must be utterly incalculable... Margate is the classical resort of the citizens of London...a very pleasant retreat from the close alleys and crowded thoroughfares of the vast and sleepless city...[10]

The day excursion and the weekend – created by the steamboat revolution – were important for the many people who did not have guaranteed holidays.

The following is a contemporary description – by an experienced traveller – of a journey to Herne Bay in October 1835, starting from the Pool of London. It is well worth quoting at length because it is illuminating for its description of the passengers:

> ...We arrived at St Kath[arine] Docks, where...[we]...embarked on board the often and justly praised *City of Canterbury*...peopled by only a few stray cits. Soon, however, more passengers descended – a fellow with a rose escorting a lady with a very agreeable pair of hazel eyes seated her and himself in amidships; a sick lady of goodly countenance was laid on the continuation of the bench, attended by her...papa; an officer in varnished boots appeared pacing the decks, which he continued to do without relaxation of muscle or feature for 4 hours by the clock, sending

The Terrace Pier at Gravesend. Engraving by J. Smeeton. *Author's collection*

his wife, son and servants to the fore part of the vessel to keep their distance as behoved them.
…the signal was given, the chimney smoked, we moved slowly from the pier of the docks, and
simmered carefully away into the intracies of the Pool, which was more than usually crowded. A
voice of command from the paddle box drew our attention to the captain, in whom we at once
recognised the original of the frontispiece and the celebrated Cap. Large of the dedication of the H
Bay Guide… The extreme caution and activity he displayed in his office showed him at once to be
a good Capn. and a conscientious man. Down we went through the Pool to the tune of 'Ease *her*',
'Stop *her*', and with all our care…running foul of a coasting vessel whose bowsprit got entangled
in our rigging.[11]

These are middle-class passengers: the self-important officer, and the gentleman with a rose.
The 'Cits' had been an object of ridicule in the eighteenth century – a tradition continued
by Dickens – often because they were regarded as social climbers. Significantly, this account
culminates in a collision between vessels in the Pool – further evidence of the congestion.

By the 1840s there were six steamship companies competing for the Margate traffic, resulting in fare reductions of almost 50 per cent. Traffic to the town had quadrupled between 1817 and 1835 – the number of passengers reached 108,625 in the latter year. As early as 1831, an MP had claimed that Gravesend, Margate, and Ramsgate had been built to cater for London commuters. The custom developed for husbands of families spending the summer season in Margate to take a steamboat from London after their offices closed on Saturday morning. These would arrive in the evening, and would be met with some excitement (or not, as the case may be) and became known as 'The Husbands Boat' or 'The Hats Boat' – about which a music hall song was written. It is not clear whether they went back on Sunday or Monday and one can only speculate on the reason for the latter name. In any case, this must have been the introduction of the 'weekend' as we know it. Here is a contemporary description (a 'story'), written by a local journalist – so some exaggeration must be allowed for:

> The number of disembarkations from the steamers at Margate alone exceeded 100,000 in the summer of 1846. On Saturdays during that season it was common to see 800 to 1000 landed there from the different steamers. But these must not all be taken as new arrivals: the male part of the visitors generally go up and down to London for their business leaving their families on the coast...[12]

And later:

> The liveliest scene at this lively watering place is on the Saturday night. There is a late steam-boat, called in the language of the place, 'The Hats boat', or 'The Husbands' boat'. The good men wind up their week's business on the Saturday afternoon, and then embark to rejoin their wives and children. All circumstances favourable, the husbands' boat ought to arrive at nine, or half-past nine, in the evening... But tides and wind will be contrary, and impede even the progress of steam... Any such delay throws Margate into a fearful state of excitement. Swoonings and convulsions take place at the Pier-head...and anxious eyes, and hands with white pocket handkerchiefs, are directed towards Reculver and the Bay...[13]

A description has survived of a trip on the *Red Rover* from Blackwall in 1844:

> We started from Cloudesley Street in a fly, and proceeded to the Blackwall Railway station, in order to take our place in the *Red Rover* packet for Herne Bay... After embarking the beautiful vessel pursued its way without interruption down the noble Thames. The numerous vessels lying at anchor from all parts of the world: the meadows sloping to the sides of the river: the gentlemen's

seats seen at a distance, with the smoothness of the water, and the beauty of the weather, made it as delightful a sail as could possibly be desired… The *Red Rover* is a most splendid vessel, both as regards its size, fittings and accommodations… Owing to the calmness of the weather we did not feel the least inconvenience from sea-sickness. We reached Herne Bay at about half past four o'clock…[14]

A written record was kept by what must have been a prosperous family travelling to Ramsgate for a three-week holiday in the summer of 1829: they consisted of a husband, wife and their child, who travelled free. They also took a servant, who, for waiting on the family, travelled at a reduced fare. During the 1820s GSNC ran advertisements in *The Times* quoting fares of 10s for servants and 12s for adults. The family were taken from Tower Stairs out to their steamer – the *Magnet* – the cost of their coach, porters, and waterman totalling 6s 6d, which was a substantial proportion of their travelling costs. They also spent money on reading material and on refreshments, and would have had to pay porters at Ramsgate for carrying their luggage. At both ends of the journey there was the problem of unregistered, thieving, porters, so the steamboat owners disclaimed any responsibility for the safety of passengers' luggage.[15]

Steamboats never became a symbol for progress in the way that railways did, but they became part of London life – probably being liked and hated in equal proportions – and became significant enough to be satirised by *Punch*. On one occasion an article alleged that Britain was over-populated and that the steamboat was a useful 'engine of destruction' which would remedy this – as effectively as smallpox:

> In proof of this, the stranger has only to trust himself on board a six-penny Gravesend boat on a Whit-Sunday. The deck crammed, and no standing room on the paddle boxes, he will be wedged in by the crowd so tightly as to preclude the use of his limbs when the accident, which is sure to occur, takes place. Exactly at the moment of the start, an opposition boat will also set off, so that the speed will be deliciously exhilarating…each captain will foul his adversary, and a few passengers will be missed from the paddle-boxes… As they will very likely amount to a dozen – quite enough to help one another – it would be nonsense to stop either vessel so the speed is doubled. In furtherance of the praiseworthy object for which these vessels were originally started (the reduction of the population) they are ordered to 'go on' at the precise moment a passenger is stepping off.[16]

This part of the story can be concluded with a trip *back* to London, for which we return to Mr Jorrocks. Having had his weekend in Margate, and lost his clothes in the process, he gets away from Margate as soon as possible – on a hoy. But the friends he came with, as can only be expected, take the steamer from the jetty on the Monday morning. Surtees' inimitable narrative is again worth quoting at length:

> Then as the hour of nine approached, what a concourse appeared! There were fat and lean, and short and tall, and middling, going away, and fat and lean, and short and tall, and middling, waiting to see them off…
>
> At the end of the jetty, on each side, lay the *Royal Adelaide* and the *Magnet*, with as fierce a contest for patronage as ever was witnessed. Both decks were crowded with anxious faces – for the Monday's steamboat race is as great an event as a Derby, and a cockney would as lieve [gladly] lay on an outside horse as patronise a boat that was likely to let another pass her. Nay, so high is the enthusiasm carried, that books are regularly made on the occasion, and there is as much clamour for bets as in the ring at Epsom or Newmarket…
>
> Precisely as the jetty clock finishes striking nine, the ropes are slipped, and the rival steamers stand out to sea with beautiful precision, amid the crying, the kissing of hands, the raising of hats, the waving of handkerchiefs, from those who are left for the week, while the passengers are cheered by adverse tunes from the respective bands on board. The *Magnet* having the outside gets the breeze first hand, but the *Royal Adelaide* keeps well alongside, and both firemen being deeply interested in the event, they boil up a tremendous gallop, without either being able to claim the slightest advantage for upwards of an hour and a half, when the *Royal Adelaide* manages to shoot ahead for a few minutes, amid the cheers and exclamations of her crew. The *Magnet's* fireman, however, is on the alert and a few extra pokes of the fire presently bring the boats together again, in which state they continue, nose and nose, until the stiller water of the Thames favours the *Magnet,* and she shoots ahead amid the cheers and vociferations of her party, and is not neared again during the voyage.[17]

The steamers, of course, caught up with Mr Jorrocks' hoy, which was becalmed, and he was hoisted aboard the *Royal Adelaide*. His jaunt to Margate ended happily.

Travellers

It is well documented that the literary giants of the period such as Surtees, Dickens, Thackeray, and Coleridge, together with, as already mentioned, the greatest of English landscape painters, J.M.W. Turner, were regular passengers from London to Margate and Ramsgate. Turner would sit alone in the stern and contemplate the sea and the sky; notoriously mean, he made himself unpopular with the waiters by bringing his own food. Samuel Taylor Coleridge recorded his impressions, saying in October 1825, how 'impossible it would have been fifteen or even ten years ago for me to have travelled and voyaged… 120 miles with fire and water blending their souls for my propulsion'.[18]

Passengers on the coastal services around Britain may have been, though not always as we shall see, lower down the social scale than those using the Continental services. The aristocracy and gentry would have been able to travel by road in their own carriages, in a leisurely way, staying at the country seats of their friends and relatives on their route. It was predominantly the commercial and mercantile classes who used the steamships – seeking orders for goods and manufactured products, making deals, and conducting a multitude of business transactions.

It was cheaper to travel by steamer than by coach, as already mentioned. For example, the steamer fare from London to Newcastle was £3 for the best cabin (in other words first class), and £2 for the fore cabin, including meals. The stagecoach fare was £4 10s inside, and £2 5s outside. Overnight accommodation and food was extra. Similarly, travel to York was cheaper if the steamer was taken to Hull, from London, for which the fare was £1 1s for the best cabin, and 15s for the fore cabin. The coach fare from Hull to York was 5s inside and 4s outside. This meant the total fare was £1 6s and 19s. If a passenger took the coach all the way from London to York the fare was £3 5s and £1 14s.[19] Passengers would also have included engineers, artisans, and tradesmen. Steamboat services were advertised in *The Times*, which must have been seen (if not always read from cover to cover) by the middle and skilled artisan classes. Services were also advertised in the provincial papers. Cargoes on the coastal trade included cured meats and provisions (groceries) and livestock.

NOTES

1 Dickens *Bleak House*, p.302.
2 Minutes of Court of Directors of St Katharine's Dock Company, 12 January 1836.
3 Whyman, *SH*, p.127.
4 Whyman, *EKS*, p.64.
5 Select Committee on Steam Vessel Accidents, p.7.
6 Bird *The Geography of the Port of London*, p.161.
7 Porter *London: A Social History*, p.186.
8 Whyman, *SH*, p.131.
9 Whyman, *EKS*, p.68.
10 mss. nd. *MLHM*.
11 Whyman, *EKS*, p.71.
12 Op. cit., p.78.
13 *Ibid*.
14 Whyman, *EKS*. p.73.
15 Op. cit., pp.70–1.

16 *Punch*, vol.2, p.183.

17 Surtees *Jorrocks Jaunts and Jollities,* p.131.

18 Lady Dorchester (ed.) 1909 *Recollections of a long life by Lord Broughton, Vol.II,* pp.133–4.

19 Jackman, pp.614–5.

CHAPTER SEVEN

'GETTING OFF OUR RIGHT LITTLE, TIGHT LITTLE, ISLAND'

After the Seven Years War (1756–1763), and the peace treaty with France, approximately 40,000 English passengers passed through Calais in 1763–64, according to Horace Walpole, grand tourist and author of the gothic horror novel *The Castle of Otranto*. The Grand Tour, the privilege of the aristocracy, came to an end with the French wars which began in 1793 and ended in 1815.[1] There were changes in the intellectual and cultural climate in Europe – the Romantic movement popularised German culture, the Rhine, and the Alps. The fascination with Italy and the Renaissance increased. The term 'tourism' was coined about 1811 conveying the idea of a circular journey – getting off 'our right little, tight little, island' as Dickens put it. In 1818 a man named Mr Emery of Charing Cross started to organise fourteen-day coach tours of Switzerland. These were well patronised and he later reduced the price from 20 guineas (£21) to £20. There was talk of a 'travelling mania' in this decade within the new middle class – a class created by the Industrial Revolution and people who had the money to travel. At first, the Alps were considered dangerous (as they were) and were viewed from the safety of the lakes, with the upper slopes left as virgin territory. By the 1840s, however, the upper slopes had been conquered, and made safe. The clear crisp air was considered therapeutic. Switzerland developed a well-organised tourist industry with efficient hotels, and parts of the country were soon well-equipped to meet the needs of the British tourist. J.A.R. Pimlott has estimated, on good evidence, that by the late 1830s, 100,000 passengers crossed the Channel.[2] The steamboat revolution facilitated this.

The first paddle steamer to have crossed to France — the *Elise* (originally the *Margery*).

The Thames linked London to Europe, and although a few services were operated from the South Coast, London was the principal port of departure for the Continent until the railways came in the 1840s.

The first steamboat to cross the Channel may have been the *Margery*, in 1816, purchased by a French company and renamed *Elise*. She sailed to Rouen, and then up the Seine to Paris where she was greeted by King Louis XVIII. As previously related, the *Caledonia* reached the Rhine in 1817. Furthermore, a steamer called the *Rob Roy* crossed from Dover to Calais, but it is not known when this significant event took place.

The first regular services from London to Calais started in 1821 with the *Lord Melville* and the *Earl of Liverpool* (168 tons) with which their owners, William Jollife and Edward Banks, formed the General Steam Navigation Co. (which will continue to be abbreviated to GSNC) and which took over the route in 1825. The journey took about ten to eleven hours; this was competitive with the route via Dover involving a coach journey from London. By 1828 the sailing time from London to Calais was down to nine hours. GSNC operated the only London–Calais service for both passengers and light cargo; the latter included valuables such as wine, silk, and millinery from Paris. In 1831, 38,695 passengers landed at Calais.[3] The total number of passengers at this time using the four French ports (Calais, Boulogne, Dieppe, and Havre) was 80,000.[4] GSNC made efforts to increase this and in 1834 (in the summer season) reduced fares to their channel stations 'in order to encourage as much as possible the prevailing disposition to Continental excursions'.[5] By 1839 the *City of London* had joined the Calais service so that, on this route, there were three steamboats running twice weekly, one mid-week, and two at the weekend.[6]

Four steamboats were operated to the Netherlands. A service to Rotterdam was started by GSNC with the *Belfast* (146 tons) and the *Attwood* (144 tons). Wigram and Green (who were principally shipbuilders) operated two steamboats to Holland called the *King of the Netherlands* and the *Queen of the Netherlands*.[7] However, by 1830 GSNC had prevailed and had purchased the latter vessel, though the directors considered her unsuitable and she was transferred from this station. Competition appeared in 1833 in the form of the *London Merchant* on the Rotterdam service, so GSNC introduced *Harlequin* to compete. Another steamer was introduced called *Batavier* which was owned by a Dutch company. The fact that departure times did not conflict with those of GSNC suggests that some kind of operating agreement may have been reached: 'they go alternately with us to Rotterdam.' Travelling conditions on the Continental steamboats varied, the weather being the chief determinant as to whether a voyage was going to be comfortable or not. The cargoes carried were also a factor: the following is a passenger's description of conditions on GSNC's *Sir Edward Banks* (180 tons) on the twenty-six-hour voyage from Holland in 1834:

> The packet had more than 60 passengers, together with their baggage and six carriages and two horses on deck – on the deck also were upwards of 100 large baskets filled with walnuts… consequently heavy and occupying that space which ought to be devoted to the crew and to the passengers. The after hold was also filled to the comings with cheese in bulk…[8]

It is therefore safe to infer that food and dairy products from Holland must have been a useful source of revenue. We know also that other light, valuable, and non-bulk cargoes from the Continent included luxury clothing from Paris (dresses, silks, ribbons etc), ormolu, *objets de mode*, and antiques. Taken to the Continent were samples of tea, cutlery, porcelain, china, and also livestock. Steam was better (even if the passengers were incommoded at times) than sail at carrying light and perishable cargoes. The trade in dairy products increased after the introduction of the steamboats.

Demand for travel to France was such that a new operator appeared: the London & Havre Steam Navigation Co. which sailed to Le Havre from about 1838 with the *Phenix* (sic). GSNC

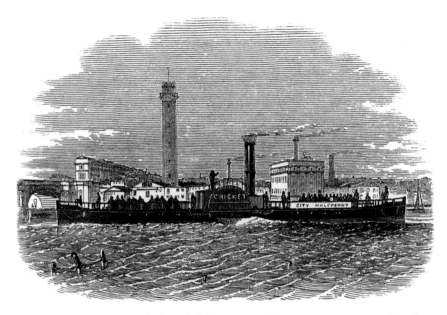

An upstream steamboat, *Cricket*, whose boiler exploded on 27 August killing seventeen passengers and severly injuring sixty, when moored at London Bridge. Her safety valve had been tied down to increase pressure. (Author's collection)

ran the *Britannia* (321 tons) and once again saw off the competition and bought out their rival in 1845, leaving them as sole operator. The *James Watt* and the *Columbine* were placed on the station to provide a twice-weekly service. This development may well have resulted in higher fares.

By 1840, Boulogne, which had a significant British community, had more than twice the number of passengers landing than at Calais – 52,807 against 20,293 – despite a journey time of fifteen hours. This may have been because it was a more attractive town, and was slightly nearer Paris. The service was enhanced by the Commercial Steam Packet Co. which operated the *Emerald* and the *Kent,* but any benefits from competition were lost when the two companies agreed to collaborate.

Hamburg, which was the most distant port from London, took fifty-four hours to reach – a great improvement on sailing ships. The *William Jollife* and the *Sir Edward Banks* operated the service when it was started by GSNC in 1826. Hamburg, one of the great seaports of northern Europe, was constantly profitable; businessmen were visiting Britain's main trading partner. There were hazards and interruptions: the Elbe froze up in winter, as did the Schelde up to Antwerp, and there were cholera epidemics. The war between Denmark and Germany in 1848 interfered with trade. The services to Rotterdam and Hamburg were subsidised by the Post Office under the terms of a mail contract from 1832. The payment was £17,000 per year but the wear and tear of winter services was considerable. Four ships were employed to serve each port.[9] By 1849 the service had been transferred to Harwich, a shorter sea route made possible because the railway from London had reached there. When the railways reached the East Coast ports and the South Coast ports' services from London declined.

A weekly service was started to Ostend in 1826. By 1828, the average number of passengers was only forty, and the sailing time was sixteen hours. This was a resort with many attractions and so it was decided to drum up more trade: in 1833 GSNC's agent was told that 'advertisements should be immediately inserted and repeated for a week and then occasionally during the month in the chief papers at Ghent, Antwerp, and Brussels that the packets run twice a week with goods and passengers'.[10] The advertising worked: by the summer of 1842 there were four services a week.[11] One of the three vessels on this station took passengers only, and GSNC was the sole steamboat operator.

Similarly, the Antwerp service was not profitable when started by GSNC in 1827, but the route became more popular in the late 1830s when steam navigation on the Rhine developed. By 1843 a service was provided by two Belgian vessels of the Antwerp Co. – the *Antwerpen* and the *PrincessVictoria* – and GSNC operated the *Rainbow*, the *Soho*, and the *Wilberforce*. The Belgian vessels sailed on Sundays and Wednesdays, and those of GSNC on Thursdays and Saturdays. So once again competition was reduced by agreement between the operators. In September 1833 an excursion to Antwerp, for two days, on the *Royal Adelaide* was advertised, weather permitting. According to the notices, tourists would be able to look at the cathedral, galleries, and visit Brussels and the battlefield at Waterloo. Dunkirk was tried: in the following year a summer service was put on but was discontinued due to lack of interest.

Four years later (1837) the destinations and the provision of services seems to have stabilised. Tourism was increasing: steam navigation on the Rhine started in 1824, and the demand for services to Antwerp increased (as already mentioned) so that GSNC bought an interest in the Lower & Middle Rhine Steamship Co. in 1835.[12] Passengers to the Rhine were told that the Antwerp route was thirty miles shorter than via Rotterdam. From Antwerp it was necessary to take a *diligence* to Cologne.[13] This was advertised as passing through 'agreeable and beautiful country' and through attractive towns such as Spa, Verviers, and Aix-La-Chappelle (Aachen). Travelling time was thirty-two hours. This was the cheapest route to the Rhine, and with the sea-crossing, meant that total travelling time from London to Cologne was down to three days. With the opening of the Antwerp to Cologne railway in 1842, a journey of thirty-two hours was being advertised in 1844 – a travelling time reduced by half.

The *Rainbow* off Antwerp. In the background is the beautiful sixteenth-century cathedral. This lithograph was made around 1845 and is by Henry Lacey. *National Maritime Museum, PAH 8857*

Passengers were notified that passage on the Rhine steamers to any place between Cologne and Basel could be obtained at Antwerp. The steamboat from Cologne to Basel took about forty hours, of which twenty-nine were spent on the boat. It had to battle upstream against the strong current, the sector from Strasbourg to Basel being the worst.

Nevertheless it was not all continuous progress: in 1841 the directors of GSNC complained about a reduction in traffic for which they blamed a variety of factors: 'stagnation in trade', the general election, and 'wintry weather' which 'restrained the disposition to travel which has hitherto proceeded in almost uninterrupted course of annual increase [sic]'.[14] Revenue picked up in the following year and *The Times* reported that there had been a substantial increase in traffic on the Rhine: in the previous year 680,000 passengers had been carried. The Netherlands Co. of Rotterdam had eleven ships, and the companies, according to *The Times*, were said to 'rival each other in zeal and attention'. This was good news for the passengers. The Netherlands Co. probably ran services from London, although they did not advertise in *The Times*, as most ship owners did. The Antwerp Co. provided services with the *Antwerpen*, which, although it had a Flemish name, had a British master – Thomas Jackson. This steamer sailed from St Katharine's Wharf every Sunday at 11.00 a.m., returning every Wednesday at 1.00 p.m. Likewise, a Belgian steamer, the *Princess Victoria*, sailed on Sunday mornings to Antwerp, at a fare of £2 2s, providing what appears to be a competitive service.

It is true to say that the development of steam propulsion to the Continent was largely due to the efforts of GSNC. By May 1844 the company had twenty-three steamboats operating to the Continent. Due to fluctuations in demand this was down to nineteen in 1846, out of a total from all operators of twenty-nine steamboats.[15] But at times demand had to be stimulated because steamboats were profitable only when they had plenty of passengers and cargo. For this reason GSNC always attempted to minimise or eliminate competition by under-cutting fares and buying out rivals. For example they reduced their fares in 1834 in order to stimulate demand, as already mentioned. In August 1837 the company went to the length of sending the mate and steward of the Calais and Boulogne steamboats to visit the 'different inns and hotels to solicit passengers.[16]

As facilities improved, tourists ventured further afield, in greater numbers, and were told that they could 'proceed by railway to Cologne, Hamburg, Berlin, Leipsig, Dresden'. The Netherland Co.'s *Batavier*, also with a British captain, sailed for Rotterdam from St Katharine's Wharf at 1.00 p.m. on Sundays. This ship was replaced by a steamer of the same name in 1855, and the service came to be known as the Batavier Line. In 1844 a new ship appeared on the Rhine – the *Elberfeld,* which had been built at Blackwall, and which cut the journey time by half: it was now possible to sail up from Cologne to Koblenz in one day. But the more daring travellers would have responded to an advertisement by the Levant Steamship Co. offering a cruise to Constantinople on *The Crescent* of 400 tons. This carried a doctor – and musicians. In the same year P&O offered cruises to Constantinople on the 900-ton *Tagus* the journey may have been more confortable on a bigger steamer, which lasted a leisurely six weeks. The *Tagus* was a paddle steamer, but by 1850 the *Nautilus*, a screw steamer, advertised as such, was sailing to Constantinople.[17] The owners must have been confident of its attraction as they did not feel the need to give any details in their notice in *The Times.* A screw-propelled steamer started running to Amsterdam. Ten years later, the Screw Steam Shipping Co. had been formed to fully exploit the new technology, and was running steamers from Irongate Wharf in the Pool to Dunkirk. These developments signified the beginning of the end of the steamboat era.

Fares fluctuated according to demand and the amount of competition, as we have noted. In May 1844 the best cabin to Hamburg cost £4 on one of five steamers: *Countess of Lonsdale*, *John Bull*, *Caledonia*, *Neptune*, and *Venezuela*, with which there were two sailings a week – not from a wharf but from midstream in the Pool (one can't help wondering if the expense of using a wharf was dispensed with because there was little competition on this service). A four-wheel carriage could be conveyed at £10, with horses at £7 each. Loading them in midstream must have been cumbersome. For shorter journeys the fares were lower – the

Steamboats on the River Elbe. The *Neptune* is entering the Elbe on passage to Hamburg, and the *Caledonia* is leaving. This a an aquatint of 1842 engraved by Edward Duncan. *National Maritime Museum, PAH 8845*

best cabin to Antwerp was £2 2s (as already mentioned) though the fare for a horse was £6. Carriages of various sizes could be taken. The once-weekly service was provided by the *Soho* and the *Wilberforce,* which sailed from Brunswick Wharf at Blackwall. By now the railway from Antwerp to Cologne and Bonn was open, which must have meant a much quicker journey. Rotterdam had two services a week provided by the *Columbine, Giraffe* (246 tons) *Ocean* (201 tons) and *William Jolliffe* (235 tons), which sailed from the Pool but called at Brunswick Wharf. The fares were the same as for Antwerp. For the French ports of Calais and Boulogne, the best cabin was 15s, and, conveniently, the steamers sailed from London Bridge Wharf, providing two services a week to Boulogne on the *Harlequin* (250 tons), *City of London,* and *Dart.* The cost of conveying a carriage is quoted as £3, though there is no mention of horses. Through bookings could be made to Paris. A similar service was offered to Calais, by the *Belfast Tourist* (236 tons), and *William Jolliffe,* the latter in between voyages to Rotterdam.

In 1836 services in the Baltic ran from Lubeck in Germany, to St Petersburg, on the Dutch *Beurs Van Amsterdam.* She sailed once a week from June to October (when the Baltic was clear of ice). Lubeck being only thirty-five miles from Hamburg meant that the journey was not onerous – even by stagecoach – and it was, of course, quicker when the

An English steamer and Vierland Ketch. This marine painting of 1856 is by the German artist Hermann Mevius (1820–1864). Vierland is the area around the river Elbe and this is a notably dramatic depiction of the estuary with the steamboat sailing either to or from Hamburg. *Altonaer Museum, Hamburg*

railway was opened in the 1860s. In 1838 GSNC notices recommended passengers to take *their* steamers to Hamburg: the *John Bull* (398 tons), *City of Hamburg* (379 tons), *Columbine* (242 tons), and the *William Jolliffe* (235 tons), and then take 'Russian and other companies' ships from Lubeck. The Russian steamers were the *Nicolai I* and the *Alexandra*, both of which had German captains and both were owned by the St Petersburg Lubeck Steam Navigation Co., and sailed weekly from May to October, enabling passengers – the company claimed – to reach St Petersburg within a week.[18] But a direct service from London had appeared by 1840: the St George Steam Packet Co. announced their *Sirius* (180 tons) sailing to St Petersburg calling at Copenhagen, which must have been for the summer only, but did not say so. Whether it was quicker is not known. This may have been the same ship which made the first steam crossing of the Atlantic in 1838. The St Petersburg passage was only possible from April to October when the Baltic was free of ice and a service started twenty years later – from Hull in 1845. There was also a weekly service from Lubeck to Copenhagen, which may have been useful for British travellers.

Four years later, in 1844, the *Mermaid* was sailing from 'off the St Katharine's Docks' to Copenhagen and St Petersburg. Then in May 1850 GSNC announced the same service on the *Trident* – a ship of impressive size, weighing 1,000 tons (her weight was actually 971 tons but this was a pardonable exaggeration) and which had good and comfortable accommodation. This had the advantage of sailing from the wharf at St Katharine's. Ten years later, in 1860, four ships were sailing to St Petersburg: *Leda*, *Adonis*, *Brenda*, and *Aurora*. The Crimean War of 1854–56 seemed to cause no interruption in trade between Britain and Russia, even though the British and French Navies blockaded the Baltic.[19] Steamship services were on offer to Balaklava and other Crimean ports to enable tourists to watch the battles; indeed, much of the Merchant Navy was employed in supplying the Army.

F.H.Pearson gives an example of the problems these diminutive steamboats experienced: sailing from Hamburg in heavy weather in October 1845 a steamer called the *Transit* had to put back to the Elbe after losing most of the cattle she was carrying. She left Hamburg again but put back to Cuxhaven two days later. She sailed on the following day but had to put back again. After two days she departed and reached Hull three days later. The ship then had to go into dry dock for an overhaul.

By September 1845, *The Times* was full of praise for GSNC.[20] It said that travel to the Continent had improved over the years only very slowly, but now the Folkestone to Boulogne steamers could be regarded as fast and efficient. GSNC had, over the years, been 'honourably distinguished by the excellence of their equipment, and by studious attention to the comfort of their passengers'. The company's new vessel, the *Triton*, was comfortable, with effective ventilation so that 'neither the heat nor the smell, generally so inseparable from steamboats, is experienced'. She had an iron hull and was put on the London to Ostend service taking twelve to thirteen hours. In the opinion of GSNC the sea voyage was not much longer than that from Dover and had the advantage of avoiding the railway journey from London. In good weather there was much to be said for this.

NOTES

1 Dr Johnson defined the 'grand tourist' as a person 'who enters a town at night and surveys it in the morning and then hastens away to another place', Hindley, p.11.

2 Op. cit., p.189.

3 *Select Committee on the Channel Tunnel*, 1883, p.189.

4 Op. cit., xxxiii.

5 Palmer *Journal of Transport History* Vol.3, No.2, p.11.

6 *Ibid.*

7 Op. cit., p.2.

8 Palmer, Thesis, p.173.

9 Palmer, Journal, p.12.

10 Palmer, Thesis, p.175.

11 Records of General Steam Navigation Co., GSN/1/8.

12 It is not stated why British ships from London did not sail up the Rhine, but Stephen Rabson of the National Maritime Museum has suggested that it was probably politically unacceptable for foreign ships to do so. I am grateful to him for this point.

13 A *diligence* was a large heavy public coach, which changed horses about every twelve miles, and covered about fifty miles a day; there were not always enough horses available, which slowed it up. It was possible to sit inside or on top and there was a coupe for the ladies, with which Ruskin's wife was delighted.

14 Palmer, Thesis, p.176.

15 Palmer, op. cit., p.164.

16 Palmer, op. cit., p.168.

17 To settle the issue, the Royal Navy arranged a tug-of-war in 1845 between a paddle and a screw steamer, which the latter won decisively. By the late 1840s iron hulls were also being introduced.

18 *Manchester Guardian*, 13 June 1838.

19 This was the first time that steamships were used in a naval action.

20 The quotations are from the edition of 12 September, p.5.

CHAPTER EIGHT

BRITS ABROAD

THE JOURNEY

Who were the tourists and travellers who benefited from the new speed and regularity of the Continental steamboat revolution? Firstly, there were commercial travellers and representatives, whose 'samples and patterns' had to be submitted to Customs (so the ship owners' advertisements stated). Secondly, there were British artisans on their way to Germany, Belgium, France, and Switzerland – helping to start up industries, including railways. In 1823 the law forbidding artisans to emigrate was repealed and these skills were exported following the industrial revolution in Britain, even though artisans' wages in London were rising in the 1820s.

A third group using the steamers were Government officials such as couriers and diplomats. And lastly and most numerously were the tourists: the Rhine castles and German Romanticism were popular amongst those of the middle classes, thirsty for knowledge and culture, as already noted. Instead of the individual aristocrat of the eighteenth century, with or without a tutor, the new middle classes started to tour the Continent after the Napoleonic wars, taking their families, including, for the first time, mothers and sisters. Of these tourists, some were educated and cultured, but 'if not seriously interested in art [they were] seriously interested in life'.[1] Travel and touring were also a means of upward social mobility – a family could re-invent themselves and pass themselves off as gentry on the Continent before returning to provincial lower-middle-class obscurity.[2]

There were also clerks, tradesmen, and numerous others who were in search of education and self-improvement. J.A.R. Pimlott describes this:

…middle-aged ladies who in the winter evenings sat at the feet of the Christian Socialist lecturers might be found exploring the Louvre at the heels of a guide, and serious-minded young clerks from the Working Men's College might be seen in their summer vacations at the end of a rope on a Swiss glacier. [3]

Tourism was still potentially hazardous and obstacles had to be overcome – language difficulties, illness, exchange rates, and passports – to name but a few. Many tourists employed their own guide and escorts – a courier, who would act as interpreter 'lest any one should strike them [the maids] dumb by addressing a foreign language to them on the road', as Dickens put it. [4]

Separate passports, i.e. visas, were needed for each country, which were obtained in London. At Calais, a British passport might be taken away and sent to Paris to be countersigned by the Minister of the Interior. The traveller would be supplied with a *passe provisoire*, which gendarmes would inspect on the road or at an inn. In Italy a local permit could be required at city gates before being accepted at an inn – and a health certificate was sometimes needed too. Amongst other advantages, the arrival of the railway led to a relaxation in French passport regulations. In 1848 the Boulogne–Abbeville railway was opened, completing the link to Paris and reducing the travelling time from fifteen to nine hours. By then many steamboat services were running from Dover and Folkestone, which had been reached by the railway from London. There was now continuous steam propulsion between the two capitals.

For those of lesser means it was made easier by the advent of the tour operator. Thomas Cook conducted his first party to France in 1855 for the Paris Exhibition. This was the break-through in foreign tours and there followed a substantial increase in cross-channel traffic. [5]

The first hazard for travellers to the Continent, if they were unwise enough not to take the steamboat from London, was the Dover road. Without cheap transport the 'trippers' walked to the coast. [6] The middle classes had wheeled transport: when, in *Little Dorritt*, the family travelled to Italy, Mr Dorritt was 'waylaid at Dartford, pillaged at Gravesend, rifled at Rochester, fleeced at Sittingbourne, and sacked at Canterbury'. [7] The descriptions in this book of the journey to Italy were based on Dickens' own experience.

Fortunately for posterity, and particularly for this book, he also recorded his impressions of his journeys to France, Switzerland, and Italy. In 1844 he bought an old stagecoach for the knock-down sum of £45 in London. When he went to Boulogne in 1856, a friend took his carriage on the steamer, which Dickens described as follows:

I found it to be perforated in every direction with cupboards, containing every description of physic, old brandy, East India sherry, sandwiches, oranges, cordial waters, newspapers, pocket handkerchiefs, shawls, flannels, telescopes, compasses, repeaters (for ascertaining the hour in the dark), and finger-rings of great value.[8]

He set off for Italy with a party of twelve, and his dog. Dickens hated the port of Calais and described it in *Little Dorritt* as:

A low-lying place and a low-spirited place Calais was… There had been no more water on the bar than had sufficed to float the packet in…the long rows of gaunt black piles, slimy and wet and weather-worn, with funeral [sic] garlands of seaweed twisted about them by the late tide, might have represented an unsightly marine cemetery…

After slipping among oozy piles and planks, stumbling up wet steps and encountering many salt difficulties, the passengers entered on their comfortless peregrination along the pier; where all the French vagabonds and English outlaws in the town (half the population) attended to prevent their recovery from bewilderment.[9]

Nevertheless he loved France and spoke French.

But Ruskin was adventuring and liked Calais. He said: 'Every traveller must love Calais, a place where he first found himself in a strange world.'[10]

The road from Calais to Paris had bilingual signs, helpfully, and there were beggars at the post-houses. The journey took two days. The roads in Belgium and Holland, in contrast to most of Europe, were good. That from Antwerp to Brussels was paved and kept in good repair. From Brussels to Ghent there was a well-engineered causeway. These two countries also had the best inns in Europe and they had the best coaches. Indeed the most luxurious form of transport was the hotel barge from Ghent to Bruges, at 1*d* per mile. It had good food with stops at canal-side taverns.[11]

Dickens' latest biographer, Peter Ackroyd, says that he was far from being the typical cockney tourist; unusually, he learnt some Italian, and may well have had more than a smattering of French. His coach trundled towards Paris which he found 'light, brilliant, sparkling, glittering,'[12] and then took the traditional route down the Rhone to Lyon, Avignon, Marseille, and then the steamer to Genoa. In a later journey, in 1853, Dickens took a different route through Switzerland: Lausanne, Geneva, to Milan and Naples. Ackroyd describes this as a standard route for the English traveller, which had 'proper' accommodation as well as 'splendid sights'.[13] They had travelled from Paris to Strasbourg on the recently opened railway, and had crossed the Alps by the Simplon pass (there were three other principal passes: St Bernard, Mont Cenis, and St Gotthard). The route from Milan to Genoa by road took thirty-one hours, and the journey from Genoa to Naples was by steamer. In fact, many travellers entered Italy by sea at Genoa, taking the steamboat from Marseille or Nice. A steamer could then be taken to Leghorn, the port for Florence and Pisa.

And this is exactly what Dickens did, once again providing us with one of his inimitable depictions of steamboat travel – in the Mediterranean. He went on from Genoa to Naples by steamboat and the vessel was known as 'the new express English ship'. The optimism was misplaced. His friend and biographer, John Forster, relates that on arrival from Marseille (the name of the ship is not revealed) she was already full of passengers, and all was in confusion. Worst of all, there were no places at the captain's table, dinner had to be taken on deck, and on top of this, no berth or sleeping accommodation was available, and heavy first-class fares had to be paid. The family party made their way to Leghorn, most decidedly roughing it. But worse fate awaited them. The ship had arrived too late to complete formalities and clear the port. Forster quotes Dickens's own words from a letter to him:

The scene on board beggars description. Ladies on the tables; gentlemen under the tables; bedroom appliances not usually beheld in public airing themselves in positions where soup tureens had lately been developing themselves; and ladies and gentlemen lying indiscrimiately on the open deck, arranged like spoons on a sideboard. No mattresses, no blankets, nothing. Towards midnight attempts were made, by means of awning and flags, to make this latter scene remotely approach an Australian encampment...

We were all gradually dozing off, when a perfectly tropical rain fell, and in a moment drowned the whole ship. The rest of the night we passed upon the stairs, with an immense jumble of men and women. When anybody came up for any purpose we all fell down, and when anybody came down we all fell up again. Still, the good humour in the English part of the passengers was quite extraordinary...

The store-room down by the hold was opened for Collins and Egg [two of D's friends]; and they slept with the moist sugar, the cheese in cut, the spices, the cruets, the apples and pears, in a perfect chandler's shop...in company with a cat; and the steward, who dozed in an arm-chair, and all-night-long fell head foremost, once very five minutes on Egg, who slept on the counter or dresser.[14]

Forster rightly calls this a 'too capital a description to be lost'.

They were spared the posting-inns which in the late eighteenth century had been described as 'shacks so infested by vermin, so that everybody had to sleep in their clothes'.[15] Italy at this time consisted of separate states, and much time was consumed negotiating with Customs officers at the constant frontiers. English tourists, everywhere in Europe, complained about fleas. They therefore took various remedies with them. To the Mediterranean they had quinine pills for malaria. French inns and hotels had communal tables, which Murray's guidebooks advised travellers not to use – for fear of eating with 'inferior commercial travellers'.[16] By the mid-century the better-off could obtain a good standard of accommodation. Ruskin and his wife stayed at the Hotel d'Albion (the name is illustrative of the English presence) in Rouen at 12f per day. For this they got a large sitting room, a bedroom, and a dressing room. On the road, they stopped at a Norman farmhouse, where they were served 'excellent coffee in bowls, roast chicken, boiled greens, cider, and for dessert, strawberries and pears'.[17]

Sightseeing

Such was the popularity of continental tourism that the *Bibliotheque Universelle* of Switzerland said in 1816 'It is raining English at present' and 'The English continue to arrive by the dozen: it is a real invasion'.[18] Similarly the *Gazette de Lausanne* reported that 'The number of Englishmen who are now living at, or passing through Geneva, is immense'.[19] The poet, Shelley, published a book describing his visit to Switzerland in 1814 in which he said of the Alps: 'Their immensity staggers the imagination…it requires an effort of the understanding to believe that they indeed form part of the earth'.[20] Who could resist this? In his book on Dickens, Angus Wilson talks of the 'awful sublimity' of the mountains which not only appealed to Dickens, but also to many Victorians.[21]

Various guides were published, the most notable being those of John Murray (already referred to), whose *Handbook for Travellers in Switzerland* went to many editions from 1838 onwards. The popularity of Switzerland had continued without remission: Murray stated that Interlaken had become an English colony 'two thirds of the summer visitors, on a moderate computation, being of our nation'.[22] J.M.W. Turner made four painting tours, the last in 1844 when he made watercolours of Lucerne, the Rigi, Lake of Zurich, Geneva, Fribourg, and the Gottard. At least ten other British artists, including Edward Lear, undertook painting tours of Switzerland at this time. It was noted in 1859 that there was a large increase in British tourists, 'many to spend their newly earned wealth'.[23] It was probable that Ruskin had had some influence – in *Modern Painters* he said of the Swiss:

You will find among them…no subtle wit nor high enthusiasms, only an undeceivable common sense, and an obstinate rectitude… They use no phrases of friendship, but they do not fail you at your need.[24]

In 1863 Thomas Cook organised his first tour to Switzerland: Dover to Calais by steamer, then from Paris to Geneva, Kandersteg, Grindelwald, and Interlaken – by railway. The tour took twenty-one days and cost £19 17s 6d inclusive. In the following year the first winter tourists arrived. Until the Romantic Movement with its interest in landscape, Switzerland had just been part of the route to Italy, and not a destination in its own right.

The Rhine was popular with the British, who preferred to travel in the 'pavilion' – a well appointed cabin in the stern of the steamer 'reserved for those who prefer a high price to a low price and will on no account travel without a partition between themselves and their inferior in wealth'.[25] The larger steamers could carry horses and carriages.

EXPATRIATES

Some tourists settled in one place for several months – as did Dickens. His servants communicated with Italians by speaking English very slowly and very loudly 'as if they were deaf rather than Italian'.[26] Dickens' cook, however, learnt enough Italian to buy food. And Mary Shelley spoke of a new generation of tourists which she called 'Anglo Italians' who understood the Italian language, were interested in the Italian people, and were independent of guidebooks. They also did not complain incessantly about local conditions. Dickens was an example – he learnt some Italian and found the ordinary Italian people delightful, though he was amused, somewhat pompously, by foreigners pronouncing English names incorrectly and getting English titles muddled. After the Napoleonic wars, Boulogne virtually became an English colony. One of Murray's guides said: 'The town is enriched by English money; warmed, lighted and smoked by English coal; English signs and advertisements decorate every shop door, in tavern and lodging-house; and every third person you meet is either a countryman or speaking our language'.[27] When residing in Boulogne, Dickens avoided other English residents; according to Ackroyd he did not care for his fellow-countrymen abroad, and cut through the 'complex and insidious bonds of Victorian etiquette'.[28] Nevertheless, his creation, Mrs Merdle, wife of the corrupt financier in *Little Dorritt*, stuck to etiquette when she gave a farewell dinner-party in Rome for the flourishing English colony: the company was 'very select' and was mainly British, 'saving that it comprised the usual French count and the usual Italian Marchese – decorative social milestones always to be found in certain places, and varying little in appearance'.[29]

Dickens' disenchanted view of the British abroad is amplified in *Little Dorrit* when the heroine reflects on the tourists which her family encounter in Venice:

> Numbers of people seemed to come abroad…through debt, through idleness, relationship, curiosity, and general unfitness for getting on at home. They were brought into these foreign towns in the custody of couriers and local followers.
>
> …They prowled about the churches and picture-galleries… They were usually going away again tomorrow or next week, and rarely knew their own minds, and seldom did what they said they would do, or went where they said they would go…
>
> They paid high for poor accommodation, and disparaged a place while they pretended to like it …they were envied when they went away, by people left behind feigning not to want to go… A certain set of words and phrases, as much belonging to tourists…was always in their mouths. They had precisely the same incapacity for settling down to anything, as the [Marshalsea] prisoners used to have; they rather deteriorated one another…and they wore untidy dresses, and fell into a slouching way of life.[30]

In Rome, with its substantial English colony, Dickens is once again disparaging – the British follow their guides and, worst of all, believe everything they are told:

> …walking about St Peter's and the Vatican on somebody else's cork legs [numb from exhaustion], and straining every visible object through somebody else's sieve… The whole body of travellers seemed to be a collection of voluntary human sacrifices, bound hand and foot, and delivered over to Mr Eustace and his attendants [the guides] to have the entrails of their intellects arranged according to the taste of that sacred priesthood. Through the rugged remains of temples and tombs and palaces and senate halls and theatres and amphitheatres of ancient days, hosts of tongue-tied and blindfolded moderns were carefully feeling their way and endeavouring to set their lips according to the received form… Nobody had an opinion.[31]

Caen, Rouen, and Avranches were also towns with sizable English communities. The lower cost of living meant that a moderate income would go a long way, and gave rise to social climbing and pretensions, as already remarked. Some English residents even tried to be taken for French, talking of their chateaux and forests, but did not succeed, it being reported that in general they had only a 'shabby-genteel appearance about them – not at all the thing'.[32]

NOTES

1 Cecil *Early Victorian Novelists,* p.20.

2 Feiffer, p.164.

3 Pimlott, p.191.

4 Dickens *Little Dorritt,* p.423.

5 Brendon, p.65.

6 Martin papers.

7 Dickens, op. cit., p.603.

8 Peter Ackroyd *Dickens,* p.813.

9 Dickens, op.cit., p.620.

10 Hindley, p.59.

11 Op. cit., p.78.

12 Ackroyd, p.456.

13 Op. cit., p.713.

14 John Forster *The Life of Charles Dickens* pp.633-4.

15 Fraser *Beloved Emma,* p.74

16 Hindley, p.63

17 *Ibid.*

18 Wraight, p.213.

19 *Ibid.*

20 Op. cit., p.217.

21 Angus Wilson *The World of Charles Dickens,* p.200.

22 Wraight, p.230.

23 Op. cit., p.250.

24 Op. cit., p.247.

25 Hindley, p.198.

26 Ackroyd, p.460.

27 Hindley, p.61.

28 Ackroyd, p.707–8.

29 Dickens, p.614–5.

30 Op. cit., p.491–2.

31 Op. cit., p.492

32 Hindley, not attributed, p.61.

CHAPTER NINE

LONDON AND ITS PORT

By the beginning of the nineteenth century the Pool of London was congested with sailing ships.[1] On the north bank were the Custom House and the Legal Quays where, from the Middle Ages, ships had been obliged to unload so that the Corporation of the City of London could collect dues. The quays and wharves on both banks of the river had insufficient space for the vessels needing them. Ships therefore had to be loaded or unloaded midstream using barges and lighters. The riverside flourished with new factories, workshops, and warehouses of all kinds. The amount of traffic had nearly trebled in the century, and then, as now, Germany was Britain's main trading partner.

A master mariner called Kenneth Beacham Martin said that the watermen's trade (see next section) of rowing passengers across the Pool was hazardous: 'there is more danger in stopping in the Pool for a passenger than in anything else'. Another witness said: 'That Pool is not to be navigated without accidents'.[2] Coal was London's main source of energy, so many of the ships congesting the Pool were colliers moored in tiers; there were no wharves or docks available for them. They were detested by those trying to steer other ships. Captain Martin said they were called 'dung craft', though one suspects this is a euphemism.[3] With so many ships of various sizes on the Thames, and with steamboats commonly racing each other, it was a densely congested and dangerous area, which got worse over time. Whereas there were nine steamers using the Pool in 1820, there were fifty in 1830.[4]

One of the best contemporary descriptions of the Pool comes from Dickens and is quoted at length. It is from *Great Expectations,* when Pip and Herbert hire a rowing boat to enable Abel Magwitch to escape from London. It is set in the 1820s:

Here, were the Leith, Aberdeen, and Glasgow steamers, loading and unloading goods…here, were colliers by the score and score with the coal-whippers plunging off stages on deck, as counter-weights to measures of coal swinging up, which were then rattled over the side into barges; here, at her moorings, was tomorrow's steamer for Rotterdam…and here tomorrow's for Hamburg…

Again among the tiers of shipping, in and out, avoiding rusty chain cables, frayed hempen hawsers, and bobbing buoys, sinking for the moment floating broken baskets, scattering floating chips of wood and shaving, cleaving floating scum of coal…in and out, hammers going in shipbuilders' yards, saws going at timber, clashing engines going at things unknown, pumps going in leaky ships, capstans going, ships going out to sea, and unintelligible sea-creatures roaring curses over the bulwarks at respondent lightermen; in and out – out at last upon the clearer river, where the ships' boys might take their fenders in, no longer fishing in troubled waters with them over the side, and where the festooned sails might fly out to the wind.[5]

In 1823 the Lord Mayor gave a warning to masters and owners of steamboats against 'excessive' speed, and attempting to overtake other steamboats. He ordered them to reduce speed when passing loaded barges and watermen's wherries with passengers.

The City Corporation issued written regulations against speed in 1825. A speed limit of 10mph was included or added to these in 1832 and an Act of Parliament ten years later attempted to strengthen these regulations. They were tightened up again in 1846 with new bye-laws for licensing steamboats, owners, and masters. How the regulations were enforced is unclear; the ship owners probably regarded them as pettifogging details that got in the way of trade. Because of complaints, speed limits were lowered to three, four, or five knots – the evidence varies – but there was little consensus or agreement, and the masters ignored them in the face of pressure from their passengers and their owners. In the summer of 1831, the superintendent of Trinity House stated that there had been thirteen recent incidents of steamboats colliding with barges. At night steamboats carried three lights; one on the masthead, one on the bowsprit, and one on a paddle box. The vessels stopped by putting the paddles into reverse, so that they were more manoeuvrable than sailing ships.[6]

From May 1835 to November 1838, twelve steamboats were seriously damaged in collisions, forty-three people were drowned and five were injured by steamboats upsetting other craft. A further seventy-two were thrown into the river, but rescued.[7] In 1836 it was decided to install marker posts at half-mile intervals along the river from London Bridge to Blackwall, and four inspectors were appointed to monitor the speed of vessels, under the supervision of the principal harbour master.[8] But it was very difficult to measure because of the force of the tide. One steamboat captain had boasted that full speed, i.e. nine to ten knots, could be achieved in one minute, an attitude hardly conducive to safety. A journalist in 1841 boasted that an iron-hulled steamer, the *Father Thames*, did the trip from the Pool to Gravesend at an average speed of 14½mph.[9] It exemplified the classic problem of safety versus speed, and steam versus sail.

A Thames pilot, Mr Taylor, giving evidence to a House of Commons Committee in 1836, complained about the speed of steamboats, saying: 'I do not consider any boats are safe when those large steam boats go up and down at the rate at which they now go', and added that 130 steamers passed through the Pool on a summer day. Captain Large testified that he had been in command of the *City of Canterbury* for two seasons and found navigating the Pool difficult, but was subject to pressure from his passengers who complained about delays – the increase in passengers to Herne Bay having been 'very great'.[10]

A House of Commons Committee asked Captain Martin how many passengers were carried by steamboats to the open sea. His reply was specific – 150 – but in the river he carried 500 to Greenwich, and 300 to Gravesend.[11] But other owners and captains had a less responsible attitude – 1,100 passengers were carried on one vessel from Gravesend on Whit Monday 1835. In an attempt to prevent overloading the City Corporation approved a bye-law limiting steamboats to carrying no more than three passengers per ton.[12]

It has been amply demonstrated that Dickens is an important source of information about the Pool, the river, and the steamboats: he drew inspiration from the Thames, and kept writing about it. In addition to his usual journeys to Margate and Ramsgate by steamboat, he chartered a steamboat to study the river and its estuary when writing *Great Expectations*. In *Sketches by Boz*, one of the comedic stories is called *The Steam Excursion* and is about a group of friends who hire a steamboat to take them to the Nore lightship in the Thames estuary (about forty-five miles from London). It is full of Dickens' acute sense of the absurd, and is worth quoting extensively:

> And then the bell at London-bridge wharf rang, and a Margate boat was just starting, and a Gravesend boat was just starting, and people shouted, and porters ran down the steps with luggage that would crush any men but porters; and sloping boards, with bits of wood nailed on them, were placed between the outside boat and the inside boat, and the passengers ran along them, and looked like so many fowls coming out of an area; and then the bell ceased, and the boards were taken away, and the boats started; and the whole scene was one of the most delightful bustle and confusion that can be imagined.

All goes well and the party have a riotous time. But when the steamboat has rounded the Nore and is heading back towards London, the weather takes a turn for the worse:

> The wind, which had been with them the whole day, was now directly in their teeth; the weather had become gradually more and more overcast; and the sky, water, and shore, were all of that dull, heavy, uniform lead-colour, which house-painters daub in the first instance over a street-door which is gradually approaching a state of convalescence. It had been 'spitting' with rain for the last half-hour, and now began to pour in good earnest. The wind was freshening very fast, and the waterman at the wheel had unequivocally expressed his opinion that there would shortly be a squall. A slight motion on the part of the vessel now and then seemed to suggest the possibility of its pitching to a very uncomfortable extent in the event of its blowing harder; and every timber began to creak as if the boat were an overladen clothes-basket.

The guests sit down to a sumptuous meal – with calamitous results:

> The throbbing motion of the engine was but too perceptible. There was a large, substantial cold boiled leg of mutton at the bottom of the table, shaking like blanc-mange; a heavy sirloin of beef looked as it had been suddenly seized with the palsy; and some tongues, which were placed on dishes rather too large for them, were going through the most surprising evolutions, darting from side to side, and from end to end, like a fly in an inverted wine-glass.

As the sea gets rougher, the excursion goes from bad to worse:

> All disguise was now useless; the company staggered on deck, the gentlemen tried to see nothing but the clouds, and the ladies, muffled up in such shawls and cloaks as they had brought with them, lay about on the seats and under the seats, in the most wretched condition. Never was such a blowing, and raining, and pitching, and tossing, endured by any pleasure party before.[13]

Dickens again. In *Martin Chuzzlewit*, the mood is different and there is a rhapsodic view of the hustle and bustle 'down among the steam-boats on a bright morning'.

> Little steam boats dashed up and down the stream incessantly. Tiers upon tiers of vessels, scores of masts, labyrinths of tackle, idle sails, splashing oars, gliding row-boats, lumbering barges, sunken piles…church steeples, warehouses, house-roofs, arches, bridges, men and women, children, caks, cranes, horses, coaches, idlers, and hard-labourers: there they were, all jumbled up together any summer morning…

A steamboat bound for Margate in the Pool, with passengers being taken out to the steamboat. This lithograph is by an unknown artist and has been dated 1820 – early days in the steamboat era. *London's Transport Museum, 3052-43*

In the midst of all this turmoil, there was an incessant roar from every packet's funnel, which quite expressed and carried out the uppermost emotion of the scene…

The press of passengers was very great; another steamboat lay on each side of her; the gangways were choked up; distracted women, obviously bound for Gravesend, but turning a deaf ear to all representations that this particular vessel was about to sail for Antwerp…[14]

This is what the befuddled nurse, Mrs Gamp, probably standing at the London Bridge Wharf, delightfully called the 'Ankworks Package'.

The London & Margate Steam Packet Co. (the 'new' Margate Co.) inaugurated the use of wharves – at London Bridge in about 1830 – which was a substantial improvement for passengers. To compete with this development the vessels belonging to GSNC (and the 'old' Margate Co.) started berthing at the new St Katharine's Steam Wharf (next to the entrance to the dock). The sleek *William IV* was the first to sail from London Bridge Wharf and the *Harlequin* was the first from St Katharine's – on 9 April that year – when it took 400 passengers for a celebratory excursion to the Nore. The wharf at St Katharine's had a frontage of 170ft and waiting rooms at each end – a significant improvement for passengers.

By 1839 there were six specialist wharves in the Pool: Fresh Wharf at London Bridge, to which GSNC and the 'old' Margate companies returned in 1835 because they were closer to the City, Hungerford, Custom House, Tower, London Bridge, and St Katharine's. St Katharine's Steam Wharf opened in 1830,[15] with an agreement to take GSNC and London & Edinburgh vessels. John Hall, one of the directors of GSNC was also a director of St Katharine's Dock Co. St Katharine's Wharf was leased to GSNC from 1846 and used for the East Coast trade.

The wharf was a great improvement for passengers; in its advertising it claimed that passengers could:

> ...embark and land, with Comfort, Personal Security, unexampled Facility, and Despatch, without the Aid, or being exposed to the Risk, of Boat-Conveyance, and also without any charge whatsoever...Persons of Rank and Distinction in particular, continue to give a decided Preference to this Establishment, not only on account of the very SUPERIOR AND PECULIAR ACCOMMODATION provided, as compared with that of any other Place at the Water-side in the Port of London, but from the circumstances also of the St Katharine's Wharf being the first to provide such inestimable Accommodation.[16]

For its services the wharf owner charged 3*d* a passenger for north Kent services, and 6*d* for Edinburgh and Continental services, though in 1839 the Edinburgh steamers were using Brunswick Wharf at Blackwall, possibly temporarily. Indeed they seem to have changed wharves constantly, possibly due to the ups and downs in demand. For excursions the wharfingers made an overall charge of £5 per steamboat.[17] The growth of steamboat services meant that by 1845 there were more wharves: Nicholson's East India, and China Wharf at Lower Thames Street – the steamboats of the (new) Star Packet Co. had started using them. Several wharves were used by GSNC in the late 1840s, with sailings from Irongate Wharf (in the Pool) to Hamburg, Brunswick Wharf (at Blackwall) to Rotterdam and Ostend, Brown's Wharf (at Poplar) to Edinburgh, London Bridge Wharf to Hull, Calais, and Boulogne, St Katharine's Wharf to Le Havre, and Wapping to Newcastle.[18] GSNC was by far the biggest single owner with their office at Irongate (on the site of the present-day Tower Thistle Hotel).

From 1829 to 1846, as many as twelve companies were operating steamboats to the Thames estuary, north Kent coast, East Coast, and the Continent. At times, in good weather at any rate, the Pool could present a picture of colour and gaiety and this was described by the *Illustrated London News* at Easter 1843:

…the river below London Bridge, whose parapets were clustered like beehives with spectators, presented a singularly animated scene. Nearly all the vessels in the Pool had hoisted their flags in compliment to the holiday – bands of music were stationed at some of the wharfs [sic] or on board the boats, and almost every minute a steamer passed deep in the water from her crowded freight of human beings. It was only by extreme caution that numerous accidents were avoided, for the highway was covered with small boats as well…and numerous coal barges… Every available corner of the decks and cabins of the steamers was occupied…[19]

A bell would be rung at the wharf to announce the departure of a steamer, with the captain standing on one of the paddle boxes shouting orders to a boy, who relayed them down a hatchway to the engineer. Here is another evocative sample of Dickens' typically sardonic description of the scene, in *Sketches by Boz*:

Coaches are every moment setting down at the entrance to the wharf, and the stare of bewildered astonishment with which the 'fares' resign themselves and their luggage into the hands of the porters, who seize all the packages at once as a matter of course, and run away with them, heaven knows where, is laughable in the extreme. A Margate boat lies alongside the wharf, the Gravesend boat (which starts first) lies alongside that again; and as a temporary communication is formed between the two by means of a plank and hand-rail, the natural confusion of the scene is by no means diminished.[20]

And from the fifth chapter of *The Old Curiosity Shop* Dickens gives us this description of the Pool in about 1840:

It was flood tide… A fleet of barges were coming lazily on, some sideways, some head first, some stern first; all in a wrong-headed, dogged, obstinate way, bumping against the larger craft, running under the bows of steamboats, getting into every kind of nook and corner where they had no business… On either hand were long black tiers of colliers; between them vessels slowly working out of harbour with sails glistening in the sun, and creaking noise on board, re-echoed from a hundred quarters.[21]

With the opening of the docks – West India in 1802, London in 1805, and St Katharine's in 1828 (the steam wharf in 1830, as already noted), the character of the Pool changed and congestion reduced – though overcrowding was used to justify the London & Blackwall railway when promoted in 1836. The use of Brunswick Wharf at Blackwall was the first instance of moving facilities downstream – a development that reached its conclusion with the opening of the container ports such as Tilbury in the second half of the twentieth century.

NOTES

1 The Pool of London is defined here as the river Thames from London Bridge to Limehouse.

2 W. Fletcher evidence to Select Committee on Steamboat Navigation, p.93.

3 Op. cit., p.12.

4 Select Committee on Port of London 1836, p3. It was estimated that by 1844 there were 200 steamboats in the river (Humpherus).

5 p.389.

6 Select Committee on Frequent Calamities by Steam Navigation, 1831.

7 Barker and Robbins *History of London Transport Vol.1*, p.41.

8 Committee for Improving the Navigation of the River Thames and Preventing Encroachments on the Said River, 14 January 1836, p.29.

9 *Herapath's Railway Magazine*, 11 Sept 1841, p.791. This steamboat and the *Sons of the Thames* were advertised as the 'fastest boats in the world'.

10 Select Committee on Steam Navigation, p.17.

11 Whyman, *EKS*, p.73.

12 Barker and Robbins, 1, p.42.

13 Dickens *Sketches by Boz*, pp.438–463.

14 Dickens *Martin Chuzzlewit*, pp.532–3.

15 *The Times*, 11 June 1830.

16 Mss. nd. MLHM.

17 St Katharine's Dock Regulations

18 F. Burtt *Cross Channel and Coastal Paddle Steamers,* p.24.

19 22 April 1843, p.269.

20 Dickens *Sketches by Boz*, p.126.

21 p.86.

CHAPTER TEN

MORE CONSEQUENCES: THE DECLINE OF THE WATERMEN

Of all the great capitals, London has the least appearance of antiquity, and the Thames has a peculiarly modern aspect. It is no longer the 'silent highway', for its silence is continually broken by the clatter of steamboats. This change has materially affected the position and diminished the number of London watermen...[1]

'Oars! Oars! Will you have any oars?' had been one of the cries of London watermen since the sixteenth century. For many centuries the river Thames was the quickest and safest means of travel in London. It was also the most efficient means of moving goods. There is no record as to when the watermen first appeared, though in 1372 the City Corporation ordered them to limit their fare between the City and Westminster to *2d* (a substantial sum at the time). In 1700 they formed into one guild or company, being the first transport workers to organise themselves in this way. City regulations required a waterman to serve a seven-year apprenticeship to become a 'free' waterman, but many evaded this.

The watermen were tough and resilient. Out in the freedom of the river they had evolved the tradition of trading blasphemies and epithets. They were famous for this ribaldry and repartee to such an extent that their company in 1761 imposed a fine of *2s 6d* (an enormous sum) for each verbal offence – the money to go to charity. Very large amounts may have been collected. The rowing boats in which they conveyed passengers were about 25ft long

A grossly exaggerated cartoon by Thomas Rowlandson, showing the watermen at Wapping and a harassed lady. Rowlandson's 'Miseries of London' were satirically based on a series of engravings by Hogarth, published in the early nineteenth century called 'Mysteries of London'. *Guildhall Library: catalogue no?*

and called wherries, and they could carry up to five people. There were steps and landing places at frequent intervals along the river.

The watermen were seriously affected by bad weather, especially ice in the river. When the river flowed more slowly and London winters were colder, the Thames froze over; in the early nineteenth century this happened in the winters of 1820–1 and 1840–1.

The steamboats brought about economic and social change – which is the principal theme of this book – and for Londoners they brought an improvement in the quality of life. But for the London watermen they brought catastrophe. Their trade had been in decline due to the new bridges: Vauxhall Bridge was opened in 1816, Waterloo in 1817, Southwark in 1819, and the new London Bridge eventually replaced the old bridge in 1831. To the detriment of the watermen, this last development enabled the steamboats to ply upstream; the new London Bridge allowed them to sail upriver from the Pool and piers were constructed for them at Nine Elms (to connect with the London & Southampton railway), Chelsea, Richmond, and Kingston. In 1830 sea-going steamboats started using the specially provided 'steam' wharf outside St Katharine's Dock. The steamboats created wash which was hazardous to the watermen. There were many accidents, and the new steam technology was bitterly resented by the watermen. In any event the river was ceasing to be the best means of getting around. London was growing rapidly, and was getting too big to walk from one side to another: horse cabs started from 1823, and the first bus was introduced in 1829.

There were still a few customers who needed to cross from one bank of the river to the other. The watermen also conveyed passengers to and from steamboats in mid-stream in their wherries. With the strong tide current and the crowding of vessels in the Pool, boarding and landing was hazardous, as noted already; another danger was the wash from the steamboats. At a House of Commons Select Committee in September 1831 MPs were told that the steamboats *Harlequin* and *Adelaide* had recently swamped a barge; a waterman gave evidence to the effect that he was swamped by the steamboat *Erin* and one of his mates drowned. The evidence of several watermen attested to the number of accidents and swampings caused by steamboats. Between May 1835 and November 1838, forty-three people were drowned by steamboats capsizing other vessels, a dozen wherries were badly damaged in collisions, and seventy-two people had to be rescued. In 1845, three men were drowned by the wash from two steamboats going at 'full speed' (probably 10–11mph). The watermen did their best to impede them and for many years after this the steamboats were targets of their delaying tactics; desperately, they rowed their wherries across the bows of steamboats to slow them down. This dangerous tactic was self-defeating as it frightened their own passengers. Captain Martin alluded to this when he told MPs that the watermen 'knowing we have power of stopping, they trifle with us'.[2] The Watermen's Co. constantly brought civil proceedings against steamboat owners for breaking the speed limit, but to little effect.[3]

Another effect of the steamers was explained by a waterman who told Henry Mayhew in 1851 that country visitors no longer hired boats for sightseeing because of the swell from the steamers:

> The good times is over, and we are ready now to snap at one another for 3d, when once we didn't care about 1s. We're beaten by engines and steamings that nobody can well understand, and wheels. [4]

The steamers had provided custom for the watermen when they had moored midstream, but the opening of wharves in 1830, had taken this away. Allegations were made that watermen solicited passengers before they got to the wharves and then took them out in to the river. It is also recorded that the river police were asked to preserve order during the disembarkation of passengers, particularly foreigners (xenophobia being prevalent then, as now).

In the late 1830s there were still 8,000 watermen.[5] They regarded themselves as skilled – possessors of a craft or trade. A seven-year apprenticeship was served, after which there was an initiation at the Waterman's Hall to become a freeman. There was a liability for service in the Royal Navy, and indeed impressment was a major problem, though two groups of watermen were excused this obligation – those already working for the Admiralty, and those working for the Lord Mayor. In the 1840s there were about 120 employed by Customs and by the police who were 'unlicensed' and not free watermen. Mayhew was told that more than half of them were literate. Their reputation for being independent and self-reliant led Mayhew to say that they were 'patient, plodding men, enduring poverty heroically, and shrinking far more than many other classes from any application from parish relief'.[6]

At Gravesend the watermen had sole rights to carry passengers on the Long Ferry, under their ancient charter. They retaliated by winning proceedings against Captain Cortis of the *Margery*, who had to be replaced by a freeman of the Waterman's Co. But this was only a temporary victory. A more effective form of retaliation was the formation of the Waterman's Steam Packet Co. which was one of the more successful operators on the river. Other watermen may have worked on upriver steamers. However, when Mayhew interviewed them in the 1840s they told him they were starving and that their livelihoods had been wrecked.

But some people did not like the watermen: in *Dickens's Dictionary of the Thames*, the visitor is warned about the Gravesend watermen in the following restrained, but unmistakable way:

> It is well to remark…that the Gravesend waterman is a personage in any dealings with whom it is desirable to keep the weather-eye open.[7]

Arthur Hayward, in his *Dickens Encyclopaedia* of 1924 describes the 'boisterous wit and coarse manners' of the watermen, and goes on to say 'It was a curious traditional custom on the river that when any two boats passed each other the boat-men [sic], and often the occupants should salute one another, though the best of friends or perfect strangers, in the vilest language they could summon for the purpose'.[8] Despite these sensitivities, one's sympathy has to be with the London watermen: they were tough and independent, performing an arduous and dangerous job.

The well-known image by Gustave Dore shows traffic conditions in the City. *Guildhall Library: catalogue no.?*

The lighters carried freight; barges carried coal, both to and from ships in the river. Because of the skill needed in manoeuvring, and the danger, lightermen were generally sober: 'A drunken lighterman...would hardly be trusted twice.'[9] They were affected by the wash from the steamboats and the worsening congestion, though the increase in freight during the nineteenth century meant greater prosperity.

It is of interest to note that Mayhew estimated that there were 20,000 casual labourers working as dockers. This was unskilled work requiring muscular strength and stamina. During his investigations, he found them to be of mixed origin – in addition to uneducated and illiterate labourers, some of them were bankrupt professionals and tradesmen struggling to stay alive. Many dockers were in dire poverty and were destitute.[10] They were paid 4*d* an hour, over an eight-hour day, or they might get a short job at 1*s* or 8*d*. A lodging house would cost 2*d* per night – without food. It was a struggle to obtain work each day as there were more men available than wanted. A change of wind might mean fewer ships and so there was even less work, resulting in starvation. As Mayhew noted, the irony was that the docks contained goods and merchandise of immense value, in an environment of great poverty.

NOTES

1 Peter Quennell (ed.) *Mayhew's London*, p.577.

2 *Special Committee on Steam Navigation*, p.12.

3 Palmer, Thesis, p.261.

4 Quennell, p.581.

5 *Select Committee on Passengers*, xxiii, 1837.

6 Quennell, p.580.

7 p.112.

8 p.153.

9 Quennell, p.582.

10 Op. cit., p.570.

CHAPTER ELEVEN
CONCLUSION

The most persistent tendency in the history of transport is creeping obsolescence. Hence the drama of the wholesale abandonment or curtailment of one form of transport in favour of another.[1]

The theme of this book has been the birth and growth of mass tourism, started by the steamboat. It produced a revolution in travel and leisure. With its timetabled services and reliability the steamboat made the 'weekend' possible. Some people had been able to afford a stagecoach, and a few travelled cheaply on the top of goods wagons, and continued to do so, but in both cases they were a minority of the population of London. Most, like Dick Whittington, just walked. The steamboats took passenger-coach traffic from the roads, especially where routes ran parallel to the coast, such as in eastern England or Kent. Many coach services were withdrawn, especially during the summer months. But the steamboats produced more feeder traffic for the coaches. Where there was a choice, the steamboats were a better option for the traveller. One minor, but probably quite important, advantage was that the ship owners did not have to pay an excise licence for the sale of wines and spirits, so alcoholic drinks were cheaper on-board. Drinking bargain wine or beer in the saloon of a steamboat must have been better than sitting on the outside (or even the inside) of a stagecoach.[2]

The steamboat enabled large numbers of Londoners, suffering from clogged lungs, to escape for the first time from the metropolis for holidays. The state of London in the mid-nineteenth century is documented graphically by Dickens in the famous opening chapter of *Bleak House* and is here quoted extensively:

LONDON. Michaelmas Term lately over… Implacable November weather. As much mud in the streets , as if the waters had but newly retired from the face of the earth… Smoke lowering down from chimney pots, making a soft black drizzle, with flakes of soot in it as big as full-grown snowflakes – gone into mourning, one might imagine for the death of the sun.

…Foot passengers, jostling one another's umbrellas, in a general infection of ill-temper, and losing their foothold at street-corners, where tens of thousands of other foot passengers having been slipping and sliding since the day broke (if the day ever broke), adding new deposits to the crust upon the mud, sticking at those points tenaciously to the pavement, and accumulating at compound interest.

Fog everywhere. Fog up the river, where it flows among green aits and meadows; fog down the river, where it rolls defiled among the tiers of shipping, and the waterside pollutions of a great (and dirty) city. Fog on the Essex marshes, fog on the Kentish heights. Fog creeping into the cabooses of collier-brigs; fog lying out on the yards, and hovering in the rigging of great ships; fog drooping on the gunwales of barges and small boats. Fog in the eyes and throats of ancient Greenwich pensioners, wheezing by the firesides of their wards; fog in the stern and bowl of the afternoon pipe of the wrathful skipper, down in his close cabin; fog cruelly pinching the toes and fingers of his shivering little 'prentice boy on deck. Chance people on the bridges peeping over the parapets into a nether sky of fog, with fog all around them, as if they were up in a balloon, and hanging in the misty clouds.

Gas looming through the fog in divers places in the streets, much as the sun may, from the spongey fields, be seen to loom by husbandman and ploughboy. Most of the shops lighted two hours before their time – as the gas seems to know, for it has a haggard and unwilling look.[3]

To repeat the point (in case one needs to), Captain Martin emphasised in 1832 the need for relief from the overcrowding, absence of sanitation, and atmospheric pollution of London:

How beneficial is this [the steamboat services] to the health of this great and populous city! Thousands embark daily on board steam vessels to inhale fresh vigour from the ocean breeze. Let us then be grateful for these advantages, procured through the medium of civilisation and science…[4]

This was the start of mass tourism. Once the basic mechanical problems had been solved and the number of breakdowns and boiler explosions reduced, the technology could be exploited by properly capitalised enterprise, and it was GSNC that was most successful in achieving this, from 1824. This was a crucial event. For twenty-five years, from 1824 to the end of the 1840s, the wooden paddle steamer, the steamboat, provided the most advanced form of transport until the steam locomotive railway took over. As the steamboats got bigger they started providing food and drink, as we have seen, and even entertainment; each year new services were introduced, new companies formed, and new steamboats with better engines built. In several respects these steamship companies were precursors of the airline industry of today: in facilitating mass tourism they were subject to price competition. As now, the treatment of passengers offered alternatives: some of the steamers ignored on-board entertainments ('no frills') and concentrated on fares and punctuality. Others made a feature of their catering: for example, the *Vesta* of 1841 was renowned for the excellence of its meals, and the *Royal William* (307 tons) went so far as to include curries on the menu. This was a novelty which had been introduced by her master, Captain Davis, an old India hand. By the 1840s one and three-quarter million Londoners were using the steamboats each year, one million landing and embarking at Gravesend. This is a huge proportion of the total London population of roughly two million (though many would have used the steamboats several times and some not at all). It means that the opportunity was taken – especially as fares got lower – to get out of the polluted, unsanitary, cholera-prone, and grossly over-crowded city, referred to above, with conditions worsening from 1820 to 1850. And it was not only to get out, but also to enjoy the sea-bathing. From the 1841 census at Margate, and from the literature of the time, especially Surtees and Dickens, we know that all those (lucky) people with a regular and reliable income benefited from this innovation.

It can be summed up by the following, extracted from *Progress of the Nation*, written by a Mr Porter, published in 1851, and quoted by Charles Capper in *The Port and Trade of London*:

> The facility of moving from place to place…has excited the locomotive propensities of the English people in a most remarkable degree. The countless thousands who now annually pass in these packets up and down the River Thames, seem almost wholly to have been led to travel by the cheap and commodious means that have been presented to them, since the amount of journeying by land has by no means lessened. The number of passengers conveyed between London and Gravesend by steam-packets in 1835 was…670,452. It was stated in evidence before a Committee of the House of Commons in 1836 that at least 1,057,000 passengers, including those to and from Gravesend, pass Blackwall in steamers every year.[5]

The transportation of large numbers of passengers, most of whom were in search of enter-tainment, led to the growth or expansion of the north Kent resorts with all the apparatus and paraphernalia of tourism – hotels, boarding houses, restaurants, theatres, music halls, ballrooms (all with their staff), street entertainers, kiosks, cabs and carriages, seamen, and fishermen with boats for hire. Employment opportunities increased substantially.

Crucially, transport patterns changed again; the railway reached Margate and Ramsgate in 1846, and Gravesend in 1849. The South Eastern Railway competed with the steamers by offering special weekend tickets – but the steamboat was still cheaper. An even bigger threat was the opening of the railway to Brighton in 1841, which as a result, became a major resort and drew middle-class and then working-class tourists from the north Kent coast. Cheap excursion trains began running to Brighton in 1844.

At least Margate and Ramsgate have survived as resorts to the present day and may be regenerated; Gravesend, on the other hand, declined, truly a victim of its own success. It lasted to the end of the nineteenth century: in 1893 *Dickens, Dictionary of the Thames* described Rosherville pleasure gardens in glowing terms. Gravesend still had four piers (it now has two) and is important for pilotage. But the excursion paddle steamer lasted, affectionately, until the Second World War; thanks to the early wooden steamboat, mass tourism was 'launched' – and expands unremittingly.[6]

Notes

1 Dyos and Aldcroft, p.53.

2 Jackman, p.615n. In 1821 coach proprietors and innkeepers on the London–Dover road petitioned the House of Commons for a tax on steamboats because of their loss of business (Humpherus).

3 Here also is a description of London fog from Dickens's *Our Mutual Friend*:

It was a foggy day in London, and the fog was heavy and dark. Animate London, with smarting eyes and irritated lungs, was blinking, wheezing and choking; inanimate London was a sooty spectre, divided in purpose between being visible and invisible, and so being wholly neither. Gaslights flared in the shops with a haggard and unblessed air, as knowing themselves to be night creatures that had no business abroad under the sun; while the sun itself, when it was for a few moments dimly indicated through circling eddies of fog, showed as if it had gone out, and were collapsing flat and cold. Even in the surrounding country it was a foggy day, but there the fog was grey, whereas in London, it was, at about the boundary-line, dark yellow, and a little within it brown, and then browner, and then browner, until at the heart of the City – which call St Mary Axe – it was rusty black. From any point of the high ridge of land northward, it might have been discerned that the loftiest buildings made an occasional struggle to get their heads above the foggy sea, and especially that the great dome of St Paul's seemed to die hard; but this was not perceivable in the streets at their feet, where the whole metropolis was a heap of vapour charged with muffled sound of wheels, and enfolding a gigantic catarrh. (Book Three, Chapter One, p.417)

4 Martin Oral *Traditions of the Cinque Ports and Their Localities* pp.22–3.

5 p.179.

6 One ocean-going paddle steamer survives – the *Waverley*, built in 1947. It is in superb condition and visits London for cruises to the Essex and Kent resorts in September.

APPENDIX A

LIST OF STEAMBOATS

Compiled from Lloyds Register of Shipping 1840 where possible, and other sources, these vessels were employed on passenger services to and from the Port of London in the period 1815 to 1860. As much information as has been documented is included:

Ship	Owner	Built	Tons	Engine(hp)	Disposal
Margery	C.E. Dodd	1814	70	10	France 1816
Victory	"	1818	n/k	n/k	Old Margate 1822
Caledonia	n/k	1816	n/k	32	n/k
Thames	Gravesend Steam Packet Co.	1815	74	16	n/k
Regent	"	1816	112	24	destroyed by fire 1817
Favorite	n/k	1817	160	40	scrapped 1831
Sons of Commerce	n/k	1817	n/k	n/k	Southend Pier Co. 1830
London	n/k	1817	n/k	n/k	John Heighington 1822
Diana	n/k	1817	n/k	n/k	1817
Hawk	n/k	1826	n/k	n/k	scrapped 1846
Rose	n/k	1832	n/k	n/k	n/k
Eclipse	Old Margate Co.	1819	n/k	n/k	scrapped 1836
Albion	"	1821	n/k	n/k	GSNC
Venus	"	1821	n/k	n/k	GSNC
Hero	"	1821	n/k	n/k	GSNC
Dart	"	1823	n/k	n/k	GSNC

Eagle	Thos Brocklebank	1820	n/k	n/k	GSNC
Royal Sovereign	"	1822	n/k	n/k	GSNC
City of London	"	1824	n/k	n/k	GSNC
Albion	GSNC	1821	n/k	n/k	scrapped 1848
Belfast	"	1821	146	n/k	n/k
Hero	"	1821	n/k	n/k	n/k
Tourist	"	1821	236	n/k	n/k
Venus	"	1821	n/k	n/k	n/k
City of Edinburgh	"	1822	301	n/k	n/k
Dart		1823	n/k	n/k	n/k
Lord Melville	"	1822	171	80	n/k
Earl of Liverpool	"	1822	168	80	n/k
Brocklebank	"	1825	126	n/k	n/k
Attwood	"	1825	144	n/k	scrapped 1853
Duke of Sussex	"	1825	n/k	n/k	sunk 1846
Harlequin	"	1826	250	n/k	scrapped 1859
Columbine	"	1826	393	140	n/k
Magnet	"	1826	n/k	n/k	hulk 1859
Sir Edward Banks	"	1826	180	n/k	n/k
William Jolliffe	"	1826	235	n/k	n/k
Merchant	"	1831	330	n/k	n/k
City of Hamburg	"	1834	379	n/k	n/k
Ramona	"	1828	278	n/k	scrapped 1853
John Bull	"	1834	398	n/k	n/k
Mercury	"	1834	n/k	n/k	n/k
Ruby	"	1834	n/k	n/k	n/k
Britannia	"	1835	321	n/k	n/k
Caledonia	"	1836	423	n/k	n/k
Giraffe	"	1836	246	n/k	n/k
Ocean	"	1836	201	n/k	n/k
Sapphire	"	1836	n/k	n/k	n/k
Leith	"	1837	494	n/k	n/k
Topaz	"	1837	n/k	n/k	scrapped 1855
Rainbow	"	1838	n/k	n/k	n/k
Prince of Wales	"	1843	n/k	n/k	scrapped 1880
Little Western	"	1844	n/k	n/k	hulk 1874
Albion	"	1848	n/k	n/k	scrapped 1887
Eagle	"	1853	n/k	n/k	scrapped 1886
William IV	New Margate	1830	n/k	n/k	sold foreign 1837
Royal George	"	1830	n/k	n/k	n/k
Royal Adelaide	"	1830	n/k	n/k	n/k
Royal William	"	1831	n/k	n/k	scrapped 1855

Emerald	Gravesend &Milton	1834	n/k	n/k	sold 1854
*Diamond*w	"	1835	n/k	n/k	scrapped 1854
Pearl	"	1835	n/k	n/k	sold 1845
Ruby	"	1836	n/k	n/k	n/k
Topaz	"	1837	n/k	n/k	GSNC
Star	Star (Gravesend New)	1834	n/k	n/k	GSNC
Mercury	"	1834	n/k	n/k	GSNC
Comet	"	1834	n/k	n/k	n/k
Planet	"	1836	n/k	n/k	scrapped 1846
Satelite	"	1836	n/k	n/k	n/k
Vesper	"	1837	n/k	n/k	scrapped 1855
Meteor	"	1844	n/k	n/k	sunk 1853
Star	"	1847	n/k	n/k	sold 'foreign' 1855
Venus	"	1854	n/k	n/k	n/k
Red	*Rover*Herne Bay Co.	1835	n/k	n/k	sunk 1852
City of Canterbury	"	1835	n/k	n/k	Waterman Co. 1854
City of Boulogne	"	1838	n/k	n/k	sold
Brilliant	Diamond Co.	1823	n/k	n/k	n/k
Essex	"	1829	n/k	n/k	sold 'foreign' 1849
Diamond	"	1835	n/k	n/k	scrapped 1854
Waterwitch	Humber Union	1835	276	n/k	n/k
Ailsa Craig	Norfolk St. Pkt	1825	171	n/k	n/k
Courier	Bird & Co	1840	n/k	n/k	n/k
Primus	"	1839	n/k	n/k	n/k
City of Limerick	Brit. and Irish	1825	304	n/k	n/k
Shannon	"	1826	325	n/k	n/k
Devonshire	"	1837	359	n/k	n/k
Duchess of Sutherland	Steam Pkt	1835	323	n/k	n/k

Duke of Wellington	Aberdeen & London Steam Co.	1829	335	n/k	n/k
Grand Turk	n/s	1837	243	n/k	n/k
Hercules	St George's Co.	1835	265	n/k	n/k
John Wood	Newc. Hamb. & Rotterdam St Co.	1831	181	n/k	n/k
Queen Adelaide	"	1831	175	n/k	n/k
Kilkenny	Pope & Co.	1837	638	n/k	n/k
Yorkshireman	Brownlow	1822	194	n/k	n/k
London	"	1825	107	n/k	n/k
Victoria	"	1837	391	n/k	n/k
Naslednick	St Petersburg Co.	1835	268	n/k	n/k
Mermaid	W&B Co. [?]	1834	259	n/k	n/k
Phenix	Havre St Co.	1838	307	n/k	n/k
Rio Doce	Rio Doce Co.	1839	212	n/k	n/k
Royal William	London, Leith Edinburgh & Glasgow Co.	1831	307	n/k	n/k
Sirius	n/s	1837	181	n/k	n/k
Vera Paz	Crozier & Co.	1835	81	n/k	n/k
Railway	London & Blackwall	1841	258	(2 cylinders)	iron hull
Brunswick	London & Blackwall	1841	n/k	n/k	iron hull
Blackwall	London & Blackwall	1841	n/k	n/k	iron hull
Eclipse	n/k	1842	n/k	n/k	n/k

n/k = not known   n/s = not stated

APPENDIX B

HOYS AND EARLY STEAMSHIPS

Commodities such as corn and fish were transported by sea from Margate to London during the eighteenth century, and possibly earlier. Hoy was a generic term (possibly of Danish origin) for small one-masted vessels (sloops) of 60–100 tons, as already noted, and these were used for this trade. Essentially they were open barges, of which there were many in the Thames. Their attraction was that the cost of transportation of goods was far lower than by road wagon (estimated to be as low as one-twelfth). According to some sources they carried thirty to forty passengers, plus cargo, and could take ten hours or three days, depending on tides and weather. The stagecoaches would take fifteen hours for the journey by road (when the sea was rough they were possibly marginally less uncomfortable than the hoys). The end to end journey of the hoy was extended by the practice of calling at any point *en route* to pick up or unload passengers and large or small consignments of goods at Gravesend, Sheerness, and Southend (for example), but they provided an important transport service for a variety of cargoes.

By present-day standards the conditions on these vessels were extremely primitive; one (unknown) writer called them a 'floating jail', yet in calm and warm weather the experience may have been pleasant. Charles Lamb romanticises them in *Essays of Elia*. With the fashion for saltwater cures at the end of the eighteenth century the demand for passenger travel to Margate increased. In response to this, 'passenger hoys' were developed by the 1790s. These could carry 100 passengers and had cabins (but of 'inferior cast' due to the low fare). By 1800 it is estimated that they carried 20,000 passengers to Margate in one year. A few beds or bunks were installed, which, it seems, were used by many of the passengers in rotation. As already mentioned, the hoys were given encouraging and optimistic names in order to reassure passengers: examples were *Endeavour*, *Fortune*, and *Good Intent*. As also noted, sailing vessels called 'tilt' boats traded to Gravesend.

The introduction of the steamboat quickly reduced the number of sailing vessels required, so that by 1822 there was only one *passenger* hoy left. The tilt boat lasted to 1833. Their role as carriers of bulk commodities and mixed cargoes continued. In the 1840s three cargo hoys were working between London and Margate, and passenger demand increased to the point where two passenger hoys actually re-entered service – though probably not for long. There was little progress in ship design in the eighteenth century, and after the end of the Napoleonic wars in 1815, British shipping stagnated. The application of steam propulsion for ocean-going cargo was slow because of the capital cost of a steamer; 50 per cent higher than a sailing ship. Added to that was the high running cost: engines and coal absorbed up to 50 per cent of the space. According to Lloyds Register of Shipping for 1840, there were 618 steamboats totalling 69,045 tons registered in the United Kingdom. In the same year another seventy-eight were built totalling 11,669 tons. In terms of average tonnage these vessels were small and many were probably tugs. So Britain dominated steam shipping: of 5,138 steamships clearing the Port of London per year in the mid-century, only 462 were foreign. Nevertheless steamboats with wooden hulls and with paddles were not the modern ship; that came with the iron hull and the screw propeller, after 1840.

The Crimean War boosted steam propulsion so that tonnage increased from 158,000 tons to 454,000 tons in the decade 1850–1860. Britain had 2,200 registered steamships in 1860 – an increase from 295 in 1830. Even so, only 10 per cent of shipping in the Port of London in 1862 was steam. Better engines were needed which did not come until the 1870s with compounding, higher pressures, and triple expansion – which reduced coal consumption. Screw propulsion replaced the paddle wheel. The opening of the Suez Canal in 1869 boosted steam – it was not suitable for sail, and it provided faster journeys to India. By 1882 the tonnage of steam had exceeded that of sail.

Few technical details of the steamboats have survived but, according to W.A. Baker in *From Paddle Steamer to Nuclear Ship,* the *Margery* had a single vertical cylinder of 22in diameter by 2ft stroke. Steam was generated at about 2psi by a flat-sided iron boiler exhausting into a condenser. The paddle wheels were 8.75ft diameter and turned at 32rpm, giving a speed of six knots.

APPENDIX C

GENERAL STEAM NAVIGATION CO.

On their formation, GSNC had proposed to operate as far afield as St Petersburg and Gibraltar. It looked impressive in their prospectus but proved to be too ambitious for the 1820s. An early trial voyage as far as Bordeaux failed.

The company's timetable stated that the company had 'powerful steam packets always ready for towing and excursions'. This was a most important role for the steamboat – they would frequently tow large sailing ships in and out of the Thames. On some of the passenger services carriages and horses belonging to passengers were shipped for free. It is not clear what the take-up on this was – Captain Martin spoke of his reluctance to take carriages (at least to Ramsgate) because of the space they consumed, but there may have been fewer passengers on the cross-channel services.[1] The evidence from Charles Dickens, already cited, is that some travellers did take their carriages to the Continent, anticipating the post-Second World War car ferry.

By 1830, in six years, GSNC had become a substantial undertaking with an office in Paris as well as London (which, as already noted, was at Irongate, next to St Katharine's Steam Wharf). Bookings for the steamers, both coastal and cross-channel, could, however, be made at various inns in the City, in common with other forms of transport such as the stagecoach, standard practice in the pre-railway age. In addition to these agents in London, they had agents at their Continental stations to handle bookings, mail and bunkers for the steamboats.

GSNC came to a useful arrangement with HM Customs in 1832 whereby their officers were given free passage from Ramsgate to London and back. This promoted harmonious relations as the company wanted to be able to land and embark passengers at the Kent port.

By 1840 the company was well established despite the ups and downs of the trade cycle, and at the half-yearly meeting, the chairman's report showed that the Board were undoubtedly satisfied with the company's performance, as this extract demonstrates:

Two General Steam Navigation Co. handbills, one dated 1826 and the other 1829. *Author's collection*

The Affairs of the Company during this period have continued to manifest that character of stability, which it has been a principal object of the Directors to secure for the Property and operations confided to their management.

Although in several branches of commerce a temporary stagnation has been experienced for some time past, yet as regards the intercourse of those Ports in whose Trade the Ships are employed, there has been, on the whole, some extension, and this extension has been attended with a corresponding improvement in the returns and the results derived therefrom. [2]

The continued 'stagnation' continued into the next year and then returned in 1847–48. By 1850 the company owned thirty-one steamers. In 1825 it bought the old East India Co. depot at Deptford (and built ships on the banks of Deptford Creek – these facilities lasted into the twentieth century) though much of the works was burnt down in 1841.

As already mentioned, the steamboat quickly proved useful as a tug, and towing was one of the stated objectives of the company. Five ships were employed in this role: *Mountaineer*, *Rapid*, *Eclipse*, *Waterloo*, and *Talbot* – all smaller than the passenger ships. [3]

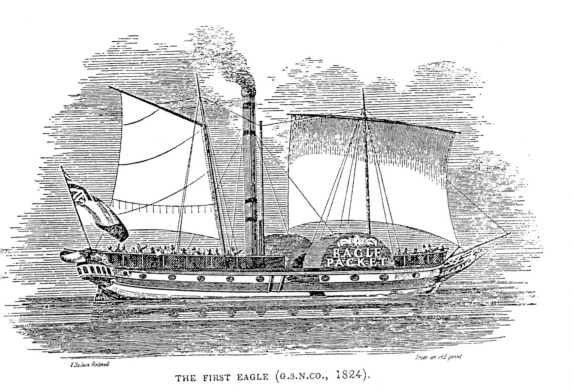

THE FIRST EAGLE (G.S.N.CO., 1824).

The *Eagle*, built at Deptford in 1820, probably with Boulton & Watt engines – few details of her have survived.
Author's collection

After the competition of the 1840s, GSNC absorbed most of their rivals on the north Kent route in the following decade. They took over the Commercial Co. in 1856, having purchased two of the Diamond Co.'s steamers – *Sapphire* and *Ruby* – two years before. Inevitably the result of this was to downgrade the route, despite the development of Cliftonville at Margate as a middle-class resort and residential area from the 1850s onwards. It is reasonable to surmise that many travellers from London would have used the new railway though it would be a mistake to suppose that the railway supplanted the steamer services. The GSNC Board recorded in 1864 that the opening of the north Kent line to Margate and Ramsgate did not 'seriously interfere with the Company's summer traffic'[4] (although the implication is that the winter traffic may have reduced).

GSNC appeared to adopt a policy of using vessels bought from other owners, though the exception was the *Eagle* of 1856 (they must have been attached to this name) – 'a very attractive and smart' vessel which remained in service for thirty years. It was followed by the *Sir Walter Raleigh* of 1862.[5] In 1871 the Bank Holiday Act was passed and this must have benefited the excursion resorts closer to London – Greenwich and Gravesend. Two years later GSNC introduced the *Hoboken* which was the first steamer to have passenger saloons on deck (i.e. as superstructure), but this apart, their fleet continued to consist of ageing steamers.

By 1850 the more recent steamers had iron hulls; the *Rainbow* of 407 tons was introduced in 1838, and was claimed to be the first iron sea-going vessel. During trials she achieved thirteen knots, and another innovation was her five watertight bulkheads. She was faster than the wooden screw-ship *Archimedes* of 1838 and could carry more cargo than a wooden ship. She firstly ran to Ramsgate, and then to Antwerp and Rotterdam. Most of the fleet was wooden-hulled. The coastal and Continental services of GSNC formed the nucleus of what is claimed to be the world's longest surviving shipping company. Having been bought out by P&O in the early 1920s, it was absorbed by them in 1971.

NOTES

1 *SC 1831,* p.17.
2 25 August 1840.
3 Palmer, *Journal,* p.4.
4 GSN 43/9.
5 This paragraph is based on the Twyman mss.

APPENDIX D

MASTERS AND SEAMEN AND THE LIFE OF CAPTAIN MARTIN

Little is known about the working life of the officers and crews of the steamboats. They worked long hours and probably had little relaxation. Mr Attwood, one of the directors of GSN professed to have a high opinion of his captains:

> [they]…are a respectable set of men; it is very essential that they should be so, for passengers are unwilling to sail unless they see in the captain a steady, capable and judicious person; they put confidence in the captain; and the capatins of these vessels are a kind of men much to be depended upon.[1]

The complement of a steamboat was: captain, mate, second mate, carpenter (very important on a wooden ship), four deck hands plus a boy, an engineer, and two firemen – this may have varied slightly, on the basis of the longer the voyage, the larger the crew.[2]

In the early days steamboats were often commanded by half-pay naval officers (the Royal Navy showed an early interest in steam propulsion). When the Humber Union advertised for a captain in 1836 they sought mariners with not only seamanship and knowledge of the coast, but 'sobriety, discipline, and gentlemanly conduct'.[3] As engines increased in size, more than one engineer or mechanic was needed, and more firemen (later known as stokers), especially on the longer routes to the Continent. The firemen had to shovel prodigious quantities of coal into the firebox. In addition to keeping the fires up they had to regulate the supply of water into the boiler and maintain steam pressure. When an engine was installed, it would be warranted for twelve months, and the manufacturer appointed the engineer, who selected his own assistants. They were not necessarily immune from seasickness and could be incapacitated, resulting in the seamen doing their work. Boys were sometimes employed – at a cheaper rate. The engineer took operational orders from the captain or pilot, such as 'Stop her'. The captain stood amidships or on one of the paddles from where he would shout his orders (sometimes with the aid of a trumpet) but very soon a gangway between the paddles was fitted (a 'bridge') from which he could give orders to the helmsman and to the engineers. There were generally four or five seamen and, of course, the steamboat carried catering staff. The living quarters for the crew were described to Mayhew as 'not fit to live and sleep in'.[4] The crew had bunks in the forecastle and in the engine room. But it was employment, and living standards ashore were low. It seems that the steamers on the Continental trade were manned with the best crews.

Evidence about wages varies: Mayhew questioned two experienced men and was told that a firemen/stoker on the Boulogne station in 1831 received wages of £1 10s per week – paying for his own food. But twenty years later a fireman said he was paid £1 4s; there was no trade union and the men could be exploited with the result that the rate may have varied from ship to ship. Labour was diluted by the ship owners by the use of boys at reduced rates, as already noted. In 1850 Mayhew was told by a seaman that on the Continental trade an able seaman got £1 per week, the fireman £1 4s, the first engineer £2 4s, the second engineer £1 15s, the first mate the same, and the captain £2 11s, or £140 a year. The apprentices were bound for five years and they got 'about £120 for the whole of their servitude'.[5] This man also complained about the accommodation on board, every part of the vessel being used for passengers and cargo. Nevertheless he felt that the wages were 'fair' and the treatment 'good'.[6]

Tobacco smuggling on the services from the Continent by the crew was a disciplinary problem for the captains, who had harmonious relationships with the Customs officers. They were expected to conduct searches if suspicious; the company could be in trouble if contraband tobacco was discovered by Customs officers.

One exceptional master mariner became prominent – Captain Kenneth Beacham Martin. He gave evidence to two House of Commons Select Committees (inquiring into Boiler Explosions in 1817 and, so important had it become, on steam navigation in 1831 – see below). He wrote two books and an unpublished manuscript. He was also a poet, and he made several oil paintings (of Ramsgate Harbour). He also kept a diary, but was not typical of his profession. Fortunately his evidence to the Committee on Steam Navigation was published for a wider audience in the *Mechanics Magazine* and most of his writing has survived. He also had a letter published in the *Nautical Magazine* in 1851 on tidal phenomena and in the same journal a letter on cork cylinders (a safety device) in 1857.

Martin was born in 1788 and went to sea in about 1809. This was the last phase of the Napoleonic wars and he saw active service in the Baltic and the Atlantic. In 1814, when it was assumed that the war was over, he was appointed to the command of a captured sailing packet, the *Wellington*, at Ramsgate, on the London service. However with the return of Napoleon and his advance towards Brussels and the Netherlands, the British Government rapidly formed an expeditionary force under the Duke of Wellington. Martin's vessel carried troops from Ramsgate to Ostend and he described this in his manuscript on Ramsgate Harbour:

No time was to be lost. The destinies of nations were at stake and England immediately put forth her iron arm to arrest the progress of her most inveterate enemy. Every vessel capable of carrying a man or horse was taken into service. No time to regard equipment usually resorted to, they were lowered into hatchways as long as they could find standing room and I took a many horses into the *Wellington* as would have been the compliment [sic] under other circumstances of a vessel three times her tonnage. Indeed the rapidity with which the British Government met this appeal to arms was truly astonishing. We had hardly listened to the note of war when the advance guard of the household cavalry were seen marching to the pier to embark. The next day I saw 34 vessels besides my own, disembarking them at Ostend. No waiting for quay berths. We put their bows upon the sand, let the horses run from the tackles into the water...[7]

The ensuing Battle of Waterloo is too well known to warrant repetition here. Martin returned to the London service, and then in 1820 two significant events occurred. He was given command of the first steamboat on the Ramsgate service – the *Eagle*. He wrote about this: 'I had every reason, in all kinds of weather, to be satisfied of her complete efficiency'.[8] He was also appointed Deputy Harbour Master at Ramsgate, a post he held until 1836, when he took over as harbour master until his death in 1859.

The *Eagle* was the first steamboat to round the North Foreland with passengers (as already mentioned). He then took 200 passengers to Calais and back on the *Majestic*, which had been built at Ramsgate. On the formation of GSNC he was given command of the *City of London*, on which he remained for the rest of his time at sea.

His first book was entitled *Oral Traditions of the Cinque Ports*, and was published in 1832. Despite the abstruse title it is easy to read; in his preface he says that his reason for writing history is 'to afford amusement (particularly among my youthful friends) by awakening their curiosity, and eliciting enquiry'.[9] One could hardly find a more laudable motive. In fact his style is clear and lucid. For him history is not academic but is a way of handing down information and ideas from generation to generation. His book is a description of the Kent coast and its harbours which he knew so well. He recalls the voyage of a hoy from Ramsgate to London from which he first saw a steamship – the *Margery* – which he then overtook, to incredulity and alarm:

Nothing could exceed the ridicule which my passengers bestowed upon this unseemly vessel; some compared her to a jaded donkey with a huge pair of panniers to its side...

I fancied (in spite of my sailor like prejudices) that I could see the future triumph of steam in short voyages.[10]

Martin describes the success of the steamboats, which in four years replaced the hoys after initial misgivings: 'our London friends swaggered as much at having made a passage by steam'.[11] Steamboats were more manoeuvrable than sailing ships and proved to be safer than sail, where there had been many accidents – some fatal – but in twelve years of steam he says he had had 128,047 passengers under his care 'not one of whom received the slightest injury'.[12]

In giving evidence to the Select Committee in 1831 Martin threw light on some of the controversies associated with steam navigation. As can be seen, one of his main concerns was with safety – or the lack of it. Steamboats went too fast in the river, but as already mentioned, passengers complained if they thought a ship was too slow. There were no regulations on navigational aids such as lights and one of the main problems was fouling barges and swamping wherries.

When asked by an MP about the loading of the steamers, he said that, in his opinion, 500 passengers could be carried to Greenwich, 300 to Gravesend, and only 150 into the open sea. The average speed of the steamers was ten knots. He said that he never carried horses (despite GSNC advertising that they would).[13] He mentioned that the steamboats on the Hamburg service (one of the longest voyages) were fitted with coal gas lighting – instead of small oil lamps. As was generally the case, the committee collected a vast amount of information, which was accurately recorded – and then did nothing. The overall problem was lack of enforceable regulation.

Martin's second book was published in 1839 when he was harbour master at Ramsgate. This had the self-explanatory title of *On the Necessity for Harbours of Refuge*. In this he took the opportunity to also campaign for better salaries and conditions for officers and crew: the better ones had a tendency to join the merchant service of the USA where the pay was good. It was Martin's opinion that those left were incompetent and prone to drunkenness.

NOTES

1 Evidence of Messrs Attwood and Brocklebank to Commissioners of Revenue, relative to conveyance of mails to [sic] Steam Packets, 1834 (xlix), p.566.

2 Op. cit., p.7.

3 Pearson, p.31.

4 Mayhew, p.322.

5 Op. cit. p.321.

6 *Ibid.*

7 Martin, *Utility of Ramsgate Harbour.*

8 Martin, *Oral Traditions,* p.28.

9 Op. cit., p.2.

10 Op. cit., p.28.

11 Op. cit., p.29.

12 Op. cit., p.30.

13 Op. cit., p.17.

APPENDIX E

DISASTERS

Here is a record of some incidents and accidents of various kinds. Safety standards were far lower in the nineteenth century than they are today:

3 July 1817: a notice was posted at Lloyds announcing the loss of the *Regent* steamer, which was bound for Margate. As already mentioned she had caught fire off Whitstable. Fortunately her captain was able to beach her and put his forty passengers and ten crew ashore. The funnel had become overheated – part of the casing had blown off in strong winds – and the decking caught fire. She had cost £11,000 to construct.

16 September 1828: according to the Board minutes of GSNC the *Columbine* struck a rock, but it is not stated where. The master, Captain Grant, was exonerated but the Board resolved to dismiss captains and officers in the event of any similar accidents in the future. This may mean that there had been similar accidents prior to this.

1831: because of complaints, many of which were justified, the House of Commons appointed another Select Committee to enquire into steamers. Several witnesses reported that steamboats fouled barges and swamped vessels e.g. wherries, in the Thames. A waterman, for example, gave evidence to the effect that he was swamped by the *Erin* in July 1831 and one man was drowned, and that the *Harlequin* (GSNC) and the *Royal Adelaide* (New Margate Co.) swamped a barge in the previous month.

August 1833: the *Talbot*, belonging to GSNC, sank in a severe gale off Ostend. No blame was attached to the master and all on board were rescued.

October 1834: GSNC's *Superb* foundered off the coast of Germany on passage to Hamburg, with the loss of all hands. She had been fitted with new engines and was regarded as a sound ship. The company paid a pension to the master's widow and £570 was raised by subscription for the families of the officers and the crew.

183?: the *Queen of the Netherlands* was lost off the Dutch coast on passage to Rotterdam due to an error by the Dutch pilot. It is not recorded as to whether there were any fatalities.[1]

1845: three men were drowned by the wash from two steamers, the *Eclipse* and the *Prince of Wales*, allegedly both at full speed.

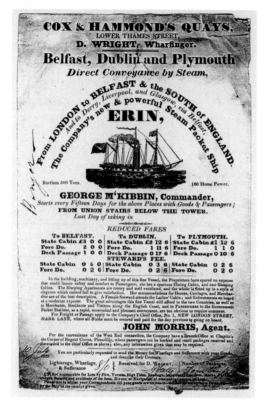

A handbill for the *Erin*. The owner is not revealed but on offer is a London–Ireland service for the summer of 1829. Erin is the ancient Celtic name for Ireland. *Author's collection*

17 July 1845: Captain Grant (name of ship not stated) put a passenger ashore at Reculver, Kent, which involved navigating a difficult channel without heaving the lead. He was strongly criticised by the Board of GSNC.

28 July 1845: the *Fame* (GSNC) grazed Dieppe Pier when leaving the harbour.

27 August 1847: The *Cricket* exploded killing seventeen passengers and severely injuring sixty. This was an 'above bridge' steamer, operating from the City to the West End, belonging to the Penny Steamboat Co.; she was moored at the landing stage (wharf) at London Bridge, and about to depart. The boiler was hurled 100ft along the river, the safety valve having been tied down to increase pressure (a not uncommon practice).

November 1851: At Margate, Jarvis' Jetty breached in severe storm. It was taken out of service and a decision to completely replace with an iron structure was taken. However, due to disagreement at Margate the new pier was not opened until 1857.

1 July 1852: Collision between the *Duchess of Kent* and *Ravensbourne* (GSNC) in a crowded river off Northfleet Point (upstream from Gravesend and opposite Grays). The former was bound for London from Margate, the latter was bound for Antwerp from London with 200 passengers and cargo. A Gravesend steamer, the *Meteor*, came alongside and passengers and crew from the stricken vessel were taken aboard just before she sank, bows foremost – 'almost perpendicularly' (rather

An artist's impression of the *Princess Alice* disaster, 3 September 1878. This event was regarded by many as being the end of the steamboat era. Illustrated London News

like the *Titanic*). It was only nine minutes from the moment of impact before she disappeared beneath the surface and therefore remarkable that there was no loss of life. The *Ravensbourne* was an iron paddle steamer owned by GSNC; the unknown owners of the *Duchess of Kent*, suffered a complete loss.

3 September 1878: the *Princess Alice* collided with the collier *Bywell Castle* and sank in Gallions Reach. She was carrying 900 passengers from Sheerness and Gravesend. As the two vessels approached each other, the master of the *Princess Alice*, Captain Grinstead, seemed unable to decide on which side to pass her. The *Bywell Castle* was empty and was high out of the water so her view was restricted. The collier's bow drove into the engine room of the *Princess Alice*, almost cutting the steamer in two. Her bow sank immediately, taking with it all those passengers sitting there. Another steamer, the *Duke of Tec,* picked up a few of the 200 saved, but 700 were drowned. It is highly probable that many died later from swallowing the severely polluted water. Public confidence in steamers was lost and patronage went into decline for several years.

NOTES

1 GSN 43/9

Appendix F

A Song: 'The Husbands' Boat'

This was on sale at 3s and was published by C. Sheard of 192 High Holborn – who also published a large number of other popular songs. The words were by F. W. Green, the music was by Alfred Lee, and it was sung, professionally, by The Great Vance. Unfortunately there is no date on the music sheet but it would probably have been in the 1850s or 1860s – when the railway had reached the north Kent coast. It demonstrates how much the steamboats had become a part of popular London life. Entertainment was provided on the steamers so it is highly likely that this was performed at sea on the voyage to Margate and Ramsgate. For anybody who wishes to see what the melody was it is in the GSN files at the library of the National Maritime Museum, Greenwich (reference GSN 41/7). The words are as follows:

Come listen to my ditty
I'm a merchant in the City
I've got a wife, the best in life
She's forty, fat, and fair
And though I love her dearly
It happened very queerly
I sent her down to Margate
As she wanted change of air

(spoken) And though I didn't want to lose the old girl – a man likes to go about sometimes – so she went by train, I meant to follow by:

(chorus)
The Husbands' boat, the Husbands' boat

Jolly old boys when we're afloat
The Husbands' boat, the Husbands' boat
For Margate in the morning

We had a loving parting
And as the train was starting
My wife called out
Don't go about to see the sights in town
Of course I said, Oh no, dear
With-out you 'twould be slow dear
So, by the boat on Saturday you may expect me down

(spoken) I kept my promise, and didn't go to more than five concert halls in one night – The Eagle,
Highbury Barn, and the National Gallery don't count of course

(chorus)
On Saturday according
The boat I soon was boarding
And with a lot of husbands got
A jolly set were we
Imagine my surprise, then
I chanced to turn my eyes
When I saw a lovely damsel
Who was looking straight at me

(spoken) Now when a wife's been away for a week, they ought'nt to allow female women on board

(chorus)
We got in conversation
I stood a cold collation
We soon got near to Margate pier
The time went quickly by
Around her taper waist, then,
My arm I had just placed
When I heard a voice
That brought me to my senses instantly

(spoken) Oh look Ma! there's father – isn't it kind of him to bring your dressmaker with him on
board

(chorus)
My feelings won't bear painting
My wife with rage was fainting
I'll draw the veil upon a scene so painfully severe

(spoken) Married men! Be careful I entreat you, your wives may come to meet you. Then take your arm away when you're in sight of Margate pier

(chorus)
My wife said 'dear, now really,
Indeed I speak sincerely
I think you'd better take the rail when you come down again'
Indeed I don't invent it
You may think that I meant it
But every Saturday, somehow, I chanced to miss the train

(spoken) So with the old girl's persuasion I returned once more to
(chorus)

MONEY VALUES
AND CURRENCY
CONVERSION

Equating historical money values with contemporary values is problematic, but since fares and salaries are quoted in this book, it may be helpful to know that the value of £1,000 in 1845 has been calculated as £55,300 in 1995.[1]

The currency of the United Kingdom was converted to a decimal system in the second half of the twentieth century, as follows:

A bill of lading from 1833 of the Dublin and London Steam Marine Co. (also called the Dublin and London Steam Packet Co.), showing freight charges for the conveyance of five boxes, contents and size unknown, from Belfast to Liverpool. *Author's collection*

119

The Pool of London in 2005, virtually empty of ships except for HMS *Belfast* (a floating museum), and a cruise liner moored to it. There is also a river bus heading upstream. Custom House is just visible but is dwarfed by new buildings at Billingsgate. London Bridge is in the background. Tower Pier, opposite HMS *Belfast*, caters for river buses downstream to Greenwich. *Photo by Bruce Rankin*

£ *s d*	12*d* (1*s*)	= 5p
	2*s*	= 10p
	5*s*	= 25p
	10*s*	= 50p
	£1	= £1

NOTES

1 See Jack Simmons and Gordon Biddle (eds) *The Oxford Companion to British Railway History*, p.579

BIBLIOGRAPHY

CONTEMPORANEOUS SOURCES

Twenty-second Report of the Commission of Inquiry into the collection and management of the Revenue arising in Ireland and Great Britain – Packet Establishment Home Stations, 1830 (xiv), 647

Corporation of London: Minutes of Committee for improving the navigation of the River Thames and preventing encroachments on the said river

Report from the Select Committee to take into consideration the frequent Calamities by Steam Navigation, and the best means of guarding against their recurrence, 1831 (xviii), 335

Report from the Select Committee on the present state of Manufactures, Commerce and Shipping in the United Kingdom, 1833 (vi), 690

Minutes of Evidence of Messrs. Attwood and Brocklebank, before the Commissioners of Revenue, relative to conveyance of mails to [sic] Steam Packets, 1834 (xlix), 566

Report from the Select Committee appointed to inquire into the state of the Port of London and to whom several petitions were referred (Navigation of the Thames) 1836. (xiv), 557

Report on Steam Vessel Accidents by Committee of Privy Council to President of the Board of Trade 1839

Report of the Select Committee on the Channel Tunnel 1883

Records of the General Steam Navigation Co., GSN series, National Maritime Museum

Minutes of the Court of Directors, St Katharine's Dock, Museum in Docklands, London

The Margate Steam Yachts' Guide, London, 1820.

The Steam-Boat Companion, or Margate Guide, London, 1823.

General Steam Navigation timetable for June 1829.

Davidsons (The Only Correct) Steam Travellers Guide n.d.

Kidd's Picturesque Steamboat Companion n.d.

A Guide to all the Watering and Sea-Bathing Places 1803

Anon *The Isle of Thanet: The Land We Live In*. c.1850. mss Ramsgate Historical Society (RHS)

Anon *Chapter Seven. The Steamers.* undated mss. Margate Local History Museum (MLHM)

Punch, Or The London Charivari, collected edn, July–December 1842

CONTEMPORANEOUS PUBLICATIONS

Cruden, R.P. (1843) *The History of Gravesend* London

Defoe, Daniel (1986) *A Tour through the Whole Island of Great Britain 1724–6* London

Dickens, Charles (1996 edn) *Bleak House* London

Dickens, Charles (1995 edn) *Sketches by Boz* London

Dickens, Charles (1972 edn) *The Old Curiosity Shop*. London

Dickens, Charles (1994 edn) *Martin Chuzzlewit* London

Dickens, Charles (1997 edn) *Our Mutual Friend* London

Forster, John *The Life of Charles Dickens* London: Chapman and Hall

Martin, Captain Kennett Beacham (1832) *Oral Traditions of The Cinque Ports and their Localities* London

Martin, Captain Kennett Beacham (1839) *On The Necessity for Harbours of Refuge* London

Martin, Captain Kennett Beacham *Utility of Ramsgate Harbour to Government Expeditions* mss

Martin, Captain Kennett Beacham (1831) *A Brief History of the Origins and Progress of the Royal Harbour of Ramsgate* mss

Morpurgo, J.P. (ed.) (1948) *Charles Lamb And Elia* London

Surtees, R.S. (1971 edn) *Jorrocks Jaunts and Jollities* London

UNPUBLISHED SOURCES

Anon Royal Eagle, *Pride of the Thames Excursion Fleet* mss. MLHM.

Anon *Miscellanea and Postscripta Facts: Memoranda of hoys and steamboats*, undated mss, Ramsgate Historical Society (RHS)

Anon *General Information on Hoys & Steamboats*, nd MLHM

Anon *Margate Steamers 19th Century*, nd MLHM

Garwood, Rev A. *Thames Steamers* mss donated in 1985 to Museum in Docklands.

Lane, Anthony Royal Eagle, *Pride of the Thames Excursion Fleet*, mss, MLHM.

Palmer S.R. (1979) 'The Character and Organisation of the Shipping Industry of the Port of London 1815–1849' PhD thesis, University of London

MacDougal, Philip *Paddle Steamer to Gravesend,* undated mss in MLHM

Twyman, Mick *Visitors By Sea, The Hoys And Steamboats,* undated mss MHS

Extracts from the Journal of Mr J Cheesewright, undated mss MHS.

PUBLISHED SOURCES

(Published in London unless otherwise stated)

Ackroyd, Peter (1999 edn) *Dickens*

Anon *Margate, A Resort History* Margate Charter Trustees. nd

Bagwell, P. (1971) 'The Post Office Steam Packets, 1821–1836, and the development of shipping on the Irish Sea' *Maritime History I*

Bird, James (1957) *The Geography of the Port of London*

Body, Geoffrey and Eastleigh, Robert E. *The London and Blackwall Railway* nd

Briggs, Asa (1982) *Marx in London*

Brendon, Piers (1991) *Thomas Cook: 150 Years of Popular Tourism*

Brobick, B. (1981) *Labyrinths of Iron – A History of the World's Subways* New York

Burtt, Frank (1934) *Cross Channel and Coastal Paddle Steamers*

Capper, Charles (1862) *The Port and Trade of London*

Cecil, David (1934) *Early Victorian Novelists*

Cornford, L. Cope (1924) *A Century of Sea Trading*

Course, E. (1976) *The Railways of Southern England: Industrial and Light Railways*

Cunningham, Hugh (1980) *Leisure in the Industrial Revolution c.1780–c.1880*

Dyos, H.J. and Aldcroft D.H. (1974) *British Transport – An Economic Survey from the Seventeenth Century to the Twentieth*

Feifer, Maxine (1985) *Going Places*

Fraser, Flora (2003) *Beloved Emma*

Gardiner, Robert (ed.) (1993) *The Advent of Steam – The Merchant Steamship before 1900*

George, M. Dorothy (1967) *Hogarth to Cruickshank: Social Change in Graphic Satire*

Girouard, Mark (1990) *The English Town*

Gurnett, Peter A.T. (19??) *A Brief History of the General Steam Navigation Company*

Hamilton, James (1997) *Turner: A Life*

Hindley, Geoffrey (1983) *Tourists Travellers Pilgrims*

Hocking, Charles (1969) *Dictionary of Disasters at Sea During the Age of Steam 1824–1962,* vol.1, A–L

Howe, G.W. (1966) 'Down River to the Sea' *PLA Monthly* June

Humpherus, Henry (1981) *History of the origin and progress of the Company of Watermen and Lightermen* vol.3, Wakefield

Jackman, W.T. (1916, repr.1962) *The Development of Transportation in Modern England* Cambridge

Kennedy, John (1905) *The History of Steam Navigation*

Kessels, S.H. (1953) 'The General Steam' *PLA Monthly* January

Lane, Leonard G. (1934) *Down the River to the Sea*

Lee, C.H. (1975) 'Some Aspects of the Coastal Shipping Trade: The Aberdeen Steam Navigation Company, 1835–80' *The Journal of Transport History* New Series, No.2, September

Martin, K.B. (1832) *Oral Traditions of the Cinque Ports and Their Localities*

Mayhew, Henry (ed. by Quennell, Peter) (1969) *Mayhew's London*

Nead, Lynd (2005) *Victorian Babylon*

Palmer, Sarah (1982) 'The most indefatigable activity – The General Steam Navigation Company, 1824–50' *The Journal of Transport History* Third Series, Vol.3, No.2, September

Pearson, F.H. (1896, facsimile reprint 1984 with introduction by Arthur G. Credland) *The Early History of Hull Steam Shipping* Hull

Pimlott, J.A.R. (1947, 1976 edn) *The Englishman's Holiday: A Social History*

Porter, Roy (1996) *London: A Social History*

Pudney, John (1975) *London's Docks*

Seaman, L.C.B. (1973) *Life in Victorian London*

Sekon, G.A. (1938) *Locomotion in Victorian London*

Simper, Robert (1982) *Britain's Maritime Heritage* Newton Abbott

Summerson, John (1978) *Georgian London*

Thompson, E.P. and Yeo, Eileen (1971) *The Unknown Mayhew*

Thurston, Gavin (1965) *The Great Thames Disaster*

Walton, J.K. (1983) *The English Seaside Resort: A Social History 1750–1914*

Weightman, Gavin and Humphries, Steve (1983) *The Making of Modern London 1815–1914*

Weinreb, Ben and Hibbert, Christopher (ed.) (1995) *The London Encyclopaedia*

Whyman, J. (1981) 'Water Communications to Margate and Gravesend as coastal resorts before 1840' *Southern History*, Vol. 3

Whyman, John (1985) *Kentish Sources, VIII The Early Kentish Seaside (1736–1840)* Gloucester

Wilson, Angus (1972) *The World of Charles Dickens*

Winter, James (1993) *London's Teeming Streets 1830–1914*

Wraight, J. (1987) *The Swiss and the British*

INDEX